Strategic
Business
Forecasting

**A STRUCTURED APPROACH TO SHAPING
THE FUTURE OF YOUR BUSINESS**

Strategic
Business
Forecasting

Simon Ramo and
Ronald Sugar

New York   Chicago   San Francisco   Lisbon
London   Madrid   Mexico City   Milan   New Delhi
San Juan   Seoul   Singapore   Sydney   Toronto

The *McGraw·Hill* Companies

1 2 3 4 5 6 7 8 9 0 DOC/DOC 0 1 0 9

ISBN 978-0-07-162126-7
MHID 0-07-162126-1

This book represents the views of the authors only and does not necessarily represent the views of any present or former employers.

McGraw-Hill books are available at special quantity discounts for use as premiums and sales promotions, or for use in corporate training programs. To contact a representative, please visit the Contact Us pages at www.mhprofessional.com.

This book is printed on acid-free paper.

|Contents

Part Two Future Possibilities

Strategic
Business
Forecasting

Introduction | **The Prediction Imperative**

Millennia ago, it is written, Joseph predicted to the Pharaoh that there would be 7 years of plenty followed by 7 years of lean. The Pharaoh embraced Joseph's prophecies and diligently employed the 7 plentiful years to prepare well for the lean ones. Doing so, the story goes, he circumvented what would have been a catastrophic famine. If this actually did happen, it has to be rated a perfect, truly inspiring, forecast-planning performance. A disastrous future possibility was foretold with specificity (7 years, not 5 or 11, and not vague), and aggressive action then was taken to benefit from the prediction and better shape the future.

Later, Julius Caesar, according to a work by a prominent playwright, was the recipient of a clear prediction when warned to "Beware the Ides of March," but he apparently chose to ignore it. He was stabbed to death on a March 15. A prediction is valueless even when accurate if not acted upon.

Today's voluminous and pervasive private and governmental predictions cover a wide range, but they do not always lead to results as valuable as those Joseph and his Pharaoh achieved.[1] At one extreme, in the category of very short-term and narrow forecasting, millions of Americans start their days choosing particular ways to get to their workplaces, opting for routes they predict will be the least congested by traffic that morning. At the other extreme, in the foretelling of earth-shaking events, few people walking city streets today would be amazed should they happen to notice a man draped in a large sign stating that the world's end is near and announcing the exact day for it.

Increasing concern about the future has led to greatly heightened interest in predicting it in virtually every category of human endeavor. Leaders of publicly held corporations are expected, and so they find a way, to make public their portents of the performances of their companies in periods ahead. Government bureaus prepare estimates of rates of inflation, interest, economic growth, productivity gains, population increases, and numerous other indicators for coming years. Thousands of financial investment professionals are occupied full-time in visualizing future rises and falls of individual securities on the stock market. Those running for political office proclaim their foresight of frightening consequences should voters elect their rivals. Some corporations assign priority to volume and imagination, rather than accuracy and reality, in their issued pronouncements about their futures with the objective of influencing their publics today.

There even are "prediction markets" in the United States where forecasts of future events are backed up with risks of cash. Business corporations—for example, GE and Hewlett-Packard— have used prediction markets to enlist the "guessing" of their employees in the forecasting of sales for new products, whether planned dates for completion of projects will be met, what will be the size of a specific product's market, and the course of many other future developments. Some companies that employ prediction markets do so applying the theories of financial journalist Surowiecki, who has claimed that groups often are smarter than the smartest people in them.[2]

In America, massive teams are busy forecasting economic trends. They do it in substantial detail about both the U.S. domestic and the international economies.[3] In fact, the key anticipated figures they publish often are presented quantitatively to several significant figures. Attempting such precise foresight involves complex computer models and is a highly sophisticated and costly endeavor—this whether the expectations are about very specialized items, like the market a year ahead for a particular truck or washing machine model or, in contrast, the future economic strength of specific nations (often China and India recently) a decade from now.[4]

Count the number of Americans engaged in gathering, analyzing, and communicating data in businesses and government, in accounting and consulting firms, and in numerous university and other nonprofit groups—all seeking trends as they predict future activities in their various fields—and the total number will reach hundreds of thousands. The expenditures accordingly amount to billions of dollars a year. Predicting is a huge business.[5]

Predictors typically do not prefer the word "predicting" to describe their work. They hate being called "prophets," "soothsayers," or "crystal gazers." They favor being described as "engaged in planning or forecasting." Managers often label a goal they wish their teams to pursue as a "forecast" or perhaps a "plan," it being what they want their staffs to strive for, not what they necessarily expect will happen. Executives may at times merely want a description of what results will follow if things continue as they are or if some particular events should occur. Thus, many different words are applied to name efforts to describe the future. No matter which word is chosen, predicting is basic to what is actually being attempted.

Those engaged in this ubiquitous forecasting are not universally admired, especially not those who describe something unbelievably bold and radical and predicted to emerge in far distant time. One who dares to prophesy the arrival of visitors from outer space risks being categorized with those who report actual meetings with visitors from outer space. Prominent scientists and engineers are always available to point out disdainfully that if we could really foresee science discoveries or technology breakthroughs, then by definition they should not be called "discoveries" or "breakthroughs." Some top economists hold in enormous disrespect other top economists who project key economic measures many years ahead. CEOs of companies that spend heavily on forecasting frequently hold their own visions of the future in high esteem, even when no more than pure hunches, while greeting their planning staff's in-depth ponderings of the future with pronounced skepticism.

With the business of making predictions a multi-billion-dollar effort in America, some participants are bound to be curious and skeptical enough to wonder whether the benefits achieved justify the high costs.[6] Many business leaders have found that the forecasters they employ can quite often do an adequate job predicting the very next quarter's results but cannot produce useful annual performance forecasts. Just as weather predictions are not always reliable when offered more than two days ahead, economists' predictions of inflation rates are likely to be badly off rather than close to the actual for a future period further away than a month.[7] Sherden has written a 300-page book full of detailed evidence proving with great clarity and high credibility that "when it comes to foretelling the future, it is sometimes hard to distinguish science from paranormal, and professional from amateur, because the track records are often so similar."[8] High-accuracy long-range predicting is virtually impossible. Even lesser-accuracy—although useful—long-range predicting is very difficult, but it has become necessary.

The main object of this book is to describe ways to predict so that the results will be worth the effort. How a business entity fares against competitors in anticipating the overall economy, market demands, technological advances, and government policy changes can spell the difference between success and failure. It is now thought too difficult to be, and risky or wrong to try to be, a successful manager without continually making serious attempts to picture what the future might bring. Although those engaged in predicting are not universally respected, it is widely felt that to lead almost any operation competently, multiple levels of forecasting effort are mandatory. Decision makers, it is believed, must prepare for future developments and not merely plan to respond when they arrive. Foresight is expected to be accompanied by appropriate advance action to maximize the positive and minimize the negative of the earlier conceived future occurrences.

Many of the predictions leaders make turn out wrong. Furthermore, the predictions, even when quite accurate, are not, and cannot always be, exploited advantageously by early activity.

But it is commonly assumed that commanders are even more likely to fail if they disdain attempts to imagine alternative futures in detail and act ahead to shape those futures.

We see then that a paradox exists with respect to predictions. On the one hand, it is not possible to foretell the most influential aspects of the future because the number of factors involved is too great and, as a practical matter, the factors are not adequately observable and measurable.[9] Equally important, the interrelationships among the numerous involved aspects are not well understood. On the other hand, to be regarded as competent, leaders must be seen as engaged in making predictions.[10] This paradox—living with it, succeeding in accomplishing intelligent and useful long-range forecasting despite its value's often being so doubtful—will be discussed in the chapters to follow. Taleb has written, "Knowing that you cannot predict does not mean that you cannot benefit from unpredictability."[11]

No university business school offers a course entitled "Principles of Prediction 101." Invite a team consisting of the most respected members of the academic world's management teachers and philosophers plus the most highly rated executives from the private and public sectors to contact us after, working together, they have succeeded in creating an intellectual discipline for predicting the long-term future and we are not likely to hear from them soon. But the prospects are often more promising when we change the request to: How can we make practical and useful predictions, given that we know the predictions will prove imperfect and often wrong, and how can we intelligently employ the results to prepare for and shape the future?

Because highly precise prognostication requires depth of understanding of the relationships among all the pertinent factors involved and the possession of rather complete underlying data—and these requirements are impossible to meet for long-term periods ahead—predicting the future is not often classified as a scientific methodology. But predicting should not be judged as totally unscientific. The scientific approach—proceeding with objectivity and logic, gathering pertinent data, observing, questioning, formulating hypotheses, experimenting to test conclusions—is not limited to efforts in which ultimate precision is the goal. Einstein is often quoted as defining science to be no more than a refinement of everyday thinking.[12] If the objective is to attain a prediction quality that, albeit imperfect, will still be beneficial, then management's bias should be to regard the ability to make competent predictions as deserving to be rated partially scientific. (It is interesting to note that, as to the predicting of scientific discoveries themselves, science fiction—often written by scientists as a hobby—has described early a large fraction of later scientific advances, from atomic bombs, black holes, and communication satellites to computers, lasers, and radar.)[13]

Forecasting can be done more productively than the way it is usually pursued today. Indeed, if we look back a hundred years and more and choose for study some of the most significant events that occurred during that period, as we shall do in the first chapter of this book, it becomes clear that too many of those events were not anticipated by leaders before they happened, and thus no suitable actions were taken in anticipation.[14] Indeed, as to past events that have most profoundly impacted our society, it seems justifiable to conclude that we could have and should have foreseen most of them, and we failed to do so. We could have and should have acted to reduce the undesirable consequences and enhance the welcome ones, and most often we did neither.

This book is in two parts. In Part 1, Chapters 1 through 6, we present methodology and procedures for useful long-range forecasting. We point out why past predictions have failed so often, and we set forth suggestions for practical approaches that will minimize failures and maximize successes. In Part 2, Chapters 7 through 16, we offer candidate predictions—future possibilities—to illustrate the applying of the recommended prediction approaches described in Part 1 for shaping the future.

Our careers have been in founding and managing high-tech corporations. This has required substantial involvement by us with governments, universities, and experts in science, technology, and finance. Our choice of examples in Part 2 of this book naturally reflects these experiences. Others who might present their views on how to make useful predictions, whose backgrounds might be in politics, art, history, law, or religion, doubtless would choose different illustrations as they discuss how to affect the future. We guess, however, that much of what we shall describe as intelligent approaches to envisage future developments will apply regardless of the fields of endeavor. Whether what you manage is a business, hospital, university department, government agency, or even a symphony orchestra or dancing school, we suspect you will find it advisable to try to prepare ahead for what might happen in the future by thoughtfully imagining possibilities and using that insight to produce superior future outcomes.

Part One | Principles of Forecasting

Chapter One | **Poor Past Predictions**

We begin our discussion of how to perform intelligent forecasting by examining the past record of predicting occurrences of great importance to society. That score, we shall find, has been so poor that it impels us to the conclusion that leaders of government and private entities must strive to be more intelligent in the future than in the past in predicting the future and shaping it. In this book we will present procedures that have worked well for us in making useful predictions. To shape the future, it is necessary to understand why leaders have done so poorly in the past. It is common, we must note, to cite poor performances in making predictions. Authors of books relating to forecasting seem often to revel in describing badly wrong predictions by others, especially when those predictors erred colossally and disastrous consequences followed (and when the predictors had been widely admired beforehand for their leadership and vision). But parading a collection of horrible past mistakes is not the object of this book. The examples of poor past predictions that we shall present were all chosen to aid in later discussion of why forecasting often has been inadequate and how to benefit from superior efforts.

In the decades closing the 1800s, a company known as Western Union was riding high. Its pioneering technology was revolutionizing the transmission of information worldwide. Having grown very large and prosperous, Western Union was a prime example at the time of how advancing technology could alter greatly and improve radically business and government operations. Western Union had turned down the opportunity to buy a new company founded by an inventor named Alexander Graham Bell. The big corporation's experts decided that "telephony" was an unnecessarily complex way to send messages, one foolishly employing human voices and ears. Fundamentally, and therefore permanently, the telephone would be limited in its transmission quality and its distance coverage. It would be costly compared with any possible advantage it might hope to offer, and it also would be extremely error prone in the critical elements of word generation and word recognition because of its dependence on those unreliable and quality-inconsistent human components. All in all, telephony, they concluded, would constitute an unsound investment by a company already possessing the proven answer to society's need for rapid and reliable communication at a distance.

Western Union's decision was an abysmal failure to envisage the future correctly. It occurred even though Western Union then housed the world's largest and most knowledgeable and experienced team in the application of technology to information transmission. Bell's company became AT&T, the world's top communication entity and one of the largest (for almost a century, the very largest) of corporations, while Western Union became increasingly minor.

Western Union was not alone in prediction failures, but it was a strong contender for the worst record among those attempting to foresee what was to come in their own specialized fields. We shall see shortly that failure to predict correctly, often even to anticipate at all, the coming of the most significant developments has been common. Indeed, those best positioned to visualize and gain from society-changing events have often erred most comprehensively.

In view of the enormous impact on the world of progress in technology, we shall describe more examples of the past record of forecasting in that category. We shall also note that poor foresight about the advent and effects of world wars served the world poorly. Prediction efforts in only these two very different areas, technology and war—and we shall describe briefly some examples in other fields as well—provide ample evidence to justify our assigning a low score to past predictions.

All now recognize that possessing the capability to exploit the progress of science and technology is necessary for a growing economy and a healthy and secure citizenry. Science and engineering advances occur continuously today through both private and government efforts. The forecasting by some individuals has been spectacularly insightful and has led to new and successful companies that grew large and became basic to the nation's gross national product (GNP). But most new companies, in contrast to their founders' and backers' predictions, fold quickly, and the established large corporations often fail to see and act on future potentials.[1] There have been far too many huge prediction errors and oversights by both government and industry leaders.

PREDICTING TV

When World War II ended, it was apparent that broadcast television had become technologically achievable. Engineers, that is, could apply new technology so that scenes in studios could be reproduced on home televisions. But would broadcast TV soon arrive? Could studio cameras, transmitters, receivers, and programs worth watching all be produced at feasible costs? Would there be enough viewers so that advertisers would pay what it would take to reach that audience? Would the timing be the near future, or would successful—that is, profitable—commercial television broadcasting be far off in time? That a serious prediction effort was needed to probe such issues clearly was indicated for any company considering a large investment to create a future television broadcast business.

One of us authors (S.R.) was employed at General Electric in 1945 (as a research scientist, not a TV broadcasting expert) and remembers well having the privilege one day of sitting in on a presentation made by GE's TV market prediction team. The team compared TV broadcasting with radio broadcasting, which was at that time a well-developed, prosperous industry producing programs reaching many millions of listeners.

The GE team explained that the price of a home TV set would be more than 10 times the price of a radio because of the much greater complexity and quantity of the TV's parts. But the number of hours a day in which typical viewers could be expected to watch their TVs would be less than a tenth of the number of hours in which typical radio listeners were listening to their radios. The team pointed out that a listener could enjoy a radio program while preparing dinner, cleaning house, knitting, driving the car, boating, dressing, performing calisthenics, painting, bathing, or making love. In contrast, a viewer must look at the TV screen. If a radio is a bit off in sound quality, only serious classical music lovers might notice or care. A picture ever so slightly off in focus or stability, however, would be totally unacceptable to every TV viewer.

The GE predictors concluded that a very high cost would be incurred in preparing programs for sight and sound as compared with sound alone. The cameras and their handling, the costuming of actors, the creating of the scenes, and the complex rehearsals would obviously be vastly more expensive than what was required for simple audio broadcasting. Even if movies were to constitute most of TV entertainment, the visual quality of the picture and the anticipated small screen of a home receiver would be noticeably inferior to what the public was accustomed to enjoying in a movie theater.

Not surprisingly then, the GE team predicted that TV would be a disastrous failure as a business. The largest electrical company in the world predicted that if TV broadcasting was ever to be commercially sound, it would have to be in the distant future when the fundamentals might conceivably somehow change greatly. So GE passed on television. (GE later did make a serious but failed attempt to enter the field.)

Perhaps we can begin to detect a pattern here. Maybe we should ask why very large and very successful companies flunk out in foreseeing the coming developments in their own areas of specialization.[2] But that is getting ahead of our story. For now we continue to describe amazing shortcomings in past predicting.

FROM LIGHT BULBS TO COMPUTERS

Well over a century has passed since electric lighting and power altered the way people live and produce for their needs. Radio and television broadcasting arrived and added more changes in the patterns of society. A number of American companies dominated these remarkable applications of electricity-based technology—notably General Electric, Westinghouse, and RCA.

The last half century saw the emergence of more electrical technology breakthroughs with vast influence on the world. Semiconductors made possible electronic computers whose arrival changed by a factor of millions (often billions) the capability and usefulness of acquiring, processing, storing, transmitting, and utilizing information.[3] Information is what makes the world's operations spin, so every activity of human beings is being transformed by the enormous expansion of information technology, be it in manufacturing, communications, banking, health care, entertainment, education, transportation, or military and civilian government activities.

The Industrial Revolution is often described as the replacing and/or the great magnification of man's physical capabilities by machines. The information revolution might be thought of as a massive extension of human brainpower. So did the large and successful electric corporations of the world predict these huge electric technology–based developments and exploit them? Did the centers of expertise in electricity see the coming of the computer age? Did they become the foremost computer companies? No. Not a single one foresaw the arrival of computers and then acted on that vision. IBM, a "punched-card" company, was not in the electronics field before the age of computers arrived; that company made itself over, becoming a new one to enter the new field. (The son of the founder of IBM, Thomas Watson, Junior, led this decision to change. IBM's founder, Thomas Watson, Senior, had predicted that there might be a national need for perhaps five or six electronic computers.)[4]

Semiconductors, the core constituents of computer componentry, replaced most vacuum tubes. Yet not a single vacuum tube manufacturer saw the future of semiconductors and acted to become a developer and supplier. What a record of strange and unintelligent predicting!

The ICBM Race

In 1953, intelligence reports added up to the astonishing conclusion—by the U.S. Defense Department (DoD)—that the Soviet Union was well along in the development of an intercontinental ballistic missile (ICBM). This perception triggered a huge crash effort to develop an American ICBM, that project becoming the largest technological development in U.S. military history (well exceeding in assigned resources the wartime Manhattan Project to develop the atom bomb).

With ICBMs, the Russians could set off nuclear explosions against the United States with total disdain for the United States' multi-billion-dollar defense system constructed to protect America from a possible manned-bomber attack. The frightening prospects of ICBMs with hydrogen bombs arriving from the USSR included not only the short flight time but also the enormous velocity of the incoming warheads zooming down from the sky. Their speed would exceed greatly that of manned bombers, and, with their high-angle trajectory, they would cause the missile's nose cone—the container of the bomb—to go unnoticed by the U.S. radar tracking system in existence at that time. That existing radar installation was able to detect manned bombers traveling over thousands of miles of land and to then instigate a U.S. response by which its interceptor planes could be launched to attack them. But that radar system would likely not detect a fleet of Soviet ICBMs carrying nuclear bombs that could destroy the United States in half an hour.

The USSR could not be allowed a monopoly of so awesome a threat, so President Eisenhower decreed that the United States must develop an ICBM system at utmost speed, and he assigned to that project the nation's highest priority.

It was utterly amazing to the DoD that the USSR could have attained an early lead on so advanced a weapons system. The Soviets had been predicted to remain far behind us technologically. For an intercontinental ballistic missile to make military sense, several key technical problems, rated then by the DoD as close to insoluble, needed to be solved. An H-bomb would do enormous damage wherever it was detonated, but the accuracy inherent in the technology then available for guiding a missile was as yet so limited that a target thousands of miles away could be missed by an unacceptable degree.

The early H-bombs were extremely heavy. Furthermore, the enormous heat generated by the payload during its streaking reentry into the atmosphere would destroy the bomb unless it was protected by a heavy blanket of material. The solution to that problem appeared to be the use of rocket engines of absurdly gigantic, hence impractical, size as the only way to boost the weighty payload into space. Moreover, the warhead and the other required apparatus (guidance and control gear, pumps, valves, and other instruments) would have to withstand terrific acceleration and vibration that, it was thought, would destroy that critical equipment.

All in all, a ballistic missile to deliver atomic bombs far around the globe was mistakenly judged by the DoD at that time as a far-fetched idea. The United States already had the "right" means for bomb delivery, the manned bomber. The DoD's faulty predicting in the early 1950s thus caused it to misjudge the ICBM possibility. The inaccurate portents aside, America and the Soviets began a furious all-out ICBM race.[5] Fortunately, the United States passed the USSR to achieve the first ICBM operational force.

What predictions then ensued? Did the ICBM capability lead to other advances? What of the possibility of utilizing space? We had learned how to loft a heavy package of equipment high above the atmosphere and to cause it to land on a precisely designated area several thousand miles away. With the planet's being spherical, what if the payload were given a slightly higher boost? Would it overshoot its target, miss Earth entirely, and become an artificial satellite? Thus, while developing the ICBM, we had automatically created the technology needed to orbit Earth.

Many promising new, advantageous applications thus were opened up. A radio signal could be directed to a receiver in a satellite whose companion transmitter could send the signal back down to a receiver elsewhere on Earth. It would become practical to telephone and to broadcast radio and TV programs intercontinentally and to direct military information and industrial, financial, medical, and every other kind of data throughout the globe via satellites.

Because satellites could be placed in highly stable orbits and also because their locations were always predictable with great accuracy, they could be used as instrumented "artificial stars" to create a breakthrough in airline navigation and to improve the navigation of ships at sea and vehicles on land.

The capability for instrumented satellites to examine Earth and transmit observations to ground stations led to obvious applications to military intelligence gathering, reconnaissance, and battle control. Earth-surface-probing spacecraft could be expected to benefit the mining, agriculture, petroleum, fishing, and forestry industries. Space-based atmospheric and surface instruments could simultaneously report on worldwide environmental conditions (temperature, moisture, pressure, tides, ocean-wave conditions, wind velocity, ice, snow, rain, fog, and so on).[6] Great progress in Earth environmental prediction and weather forecasting would result.

A host of major industrial corporations in the United States—airplane companies, electric and electronics equipment manufacturers, chemicals producers, instrument makers, and numerous apparatus specialists—were involved in the huge ICBM program, and all should have noted these future space-based possibilities. Surprisingly, however, only one company—TRW—predicted that a "space race" would occur and that a space technology industry build-up would follow.[7] TRW's prediction led it to take on the risk of creating an expensive special facility to design, produce, and test spacecraft. This anticipatory effort was rewarded by that company's becoming the first, and to this day a leading, producer of spacecraft for the DoD and NASA. (The U.S. Space Foundation, in its annual Space Report issued in 2006, estimated that the space economy added up to $180 billion in 2005, 60 percent coming from commercial goods and services.)[8]

THE USSR's *SPUTNIK*

Why had the United States not predicted Russia's *Sputnik* and instead been so shaken when it happened? The United States earlier had announced it would send into orbit a very small instrumented capsule by 1958 as part of the so-called International Geophysical Year (IGY). The idea had arisen early of assigning the producing and orbiting of that IGY satellite to the ICBM team, which was so large an assembly of pertinent engineering talent and installed resources that it would have been a tiny added chore to loft that small package. When the IGY plans were being developed, however, America's ICBM program was the nation's highest-priority project. Also, it was a secret at the time that the United States even had an ICBM program, and adding the satellite project of the IGY, an internationally open program, to the ICBM team would disclose that team's existence. The DoD would not countenance even a trivial delay in the ICBM's operational date to accommodate what they saw as a minor science project.

The Soviet Union was behind the United States in the efficiency of its nuclear bombs and in its electronics, so it had to design its ICBM to carry a much heavier payload. This mandated correspondingly larger rocket engines. The Soviet Union's ICBM consequently could boost a greater weight into orbit than could America's. Having this knowledge by itself would not have been enough for the United States to predict an early *Sputnik* launch. But there was more. Although the IGY was a multinational science program, it had been planned under U.S. leadership. The Soviet Union's contribution was wrongly predicted to be minor, befitting a nation backward in science and technology. It should have been foreseen that the Soviets might resent that rating and find it irresistible to shame the United States' little IGY instrument package by orbiting a much larger payload and doing it earlier.

As it was, the *Sputnik* launch amazed the world and shocked the United States. We were accustomed to the Russians' excelling in vodka, ballet, and caviar, but we had expected to be the first to launch an artificial moon. The Soviet's *Sputnik* offended and alarmed us. America responded and the Space Race began. The United States created a new government agency, the National Aeronautics and Space Administration (NASA), which was prestigious and reported directly to the president.

EASY AND SILLY PREDICTIONS

In the foregoing discussion, we have called attention to failures to predict highly important societal changes based on advancements in technology and science. We noted misses by those forecasters who might have been expected to predict well because their previously successful activities made them the most knowledgeable experts in their specific fields. There is another extreme. It is the category of experts' predictions of technological advances that never occurred. We cite a few of these nonevents.

When nuclear phenomena came to be understood sufficiently to enable the production of enormously powerful bombs and commercial electric power, predictions were made that we would soon be flying nuclear powered airplanes not needing refueling more often than once a year. Nuclear powered autos would make gas stations obsolete. A Pan Am airline executive, shortly after the first landings of U.S. astronauts on the moon, announced that he was getting ready to take advanced orders for lunar visits. (That airline went out of business in 1991.) Permanent colonies of Earth people on Mars are continually predicted today. Some futurists have claimed we will learn how to send electromagnetic waves into our brains while sleeping so as to become educated. After we succeeded in mapping and sequencing the human genome, some predicted we would soon eliminate disease and stop aging.

Perhaps some elements of these predictions may be realized in the future, but no evidence justified such prognostications when they were made.

THE FAILURE TO FORESEE WARFARE

Anyone reading the works of top historians, or the Bible, will find a good fraction of the pages to be about wars. Did the leaders of clans and nations envisage that the wars they started might not go as anticipated? Let us look back over the past two centuries and see if we can gauge the quality of predicting between then and now.

Napoleon must have had firm confidence in his foretelling of victory—while he was winning. His prediction score sank, however, when he invaded Russia; his prognostications did not include returning almost alone, most of his troops having been lost in that disaster. Hitler topped that. He predicted to the world that his Third Reich would last 1,000 years, a forecast off by roughly 990. He wrongly foresaw victory when, like Napoleon, he set out to conquer Russia. That bit of forecasting, critical to his plans, was all the more deserving of the term "unintelligent" because Napoleon's adventuring in that same region was still so well remembered.

The foresight by Great Britain's prime minister Neville Chamberlain of the infamous "Peace in Our Time"—this after he so wrongly prognosticated that appeasement would satisfy Hitler—makes that Englishman the leading candidate for worst predictor of the twentieth century. A challenger to that title in the category of British prime ministers would be Stanley Baldwin, who preceded Chamberlain and did essentially nothing while Hitler was creating a powerful army. The leaders of France, before World War II, were competitive with the prime ministers of England in their failure to see ahead and shape the future so as to prevent that war.

In contrast, Winston Churchill was extraordinarily accurate when he originally began to see Hitler's actions ahead of time.[9] Unfortunately, he was not then the leader of the United Kingdom's government. Historians studying the Franklin Roosevelt period in America have provided us with ample evidence that FDR foresaw the United States' need to enter World War II but was delayed in acting on his accurate foresight because of counter, and wrong, forecasting by the American Congress and public.[10] The majority thought the United States could stay aloof from that conflict.

Back before World War I, many individuals of high world standing and influence predicted that a major world war could not happen. Their reason? International trade and investment in Europe had reached an unprecedented level, the Industrial Revolution's having taken off with high momentum and depth. The rapid growth of the interlocked economies of Britain, Germany, Austria, France, and Russia had risen to enormous importance, so any war threatening their prosperity, the predictors were certain, would be successfully ruled out by the closely cooperating and powerful bankers and leading industrialists of those countries. Moreover, the European nations' then influential royal leaders were relatives—the Kaiser, for example, was Queen Victoria's nephew—who wanted no war against each other. Before World War I, to cite an example of confidence that a no-more-war era had begun, the leaders of the Austro-Hungarian Empire built an enormous array of massive government buildings in Vienna, and those buildings were designed to last forever and be the headquarters of, and an impressive symbol of, a permanent empire. That empire was destroyed in the war, an event far from the predictions of its leadership.

Of course, the most recent example of a wrong prediction with respect to war is the forecast of U.S. troops being welcomed in Iraq.

POSTWAR PREDICTIONS

At the close of World War II when the Soviet Union and the Allies were sharing control of Germany, what did most predict for that country? Certainly not that (former Nazi) West Germany would become a stable, peaceful, and prosperous democracy.[11] The main predictors of Japan's future after World War II ended were equally badly mistaken. They argued that for this previously emperor- and military-led country—after being ruled (they wrongly assumed highly resentfully) for years by the United States' military superstar, General MacArthur—to become an economically robust democracy was an absurd expectation.

In the Vietnam War, the worst of several illustrations of bad predicting was the anticipation of early victory leading to the United States' control of Southeast Asia, and with that the elimination of the communist threat there. The enormous gap between the expected events and the actual events continued right to the end when the American forces were forced to depart Vietnam in a horrible, hurried frenzy, evidencing an extreme lack of foresight and hence a lack of preparing for that awful finish.

JAPAN, INC.

We all remember "Japan, Inc.," a name that symbolized the widely held prediction that Japan's rapid economic growth in the 1960s and 1970s—what with Japan's capture of world markets for its electronics, autos, and trucks and the growing U.S. trade deficit with Japan—would challenge the American economy's leadership. Japan was predicted by many to become the No. 1 world power because it was utilizing a mysterious, brilliant strategy. Japan's financial institutions, government, manufacturing corporations, and savings-intent citizens were all seen to be working together amazingly tightly to accomplish this. As the 1970s moved into the 1980s and 1990s, however, this prediction proved enormously faulty. Japan was embarrassed when it became apparent that it was using its dollar surplus to vastly overpay for U.S. and other real estate, the income from which was far below its forecasts, creating a major credit crisis.

Sony, then the Japanese company most often cited to illustrate Japan's takeover of world markets by its supremacy in management, ran into very bad performance troubles. Sony is now led by a non-Japanese, foreign-born CEO. Japan's Nissan Motors encountered a similarly unanticipated circumstance.

The Fall of the USSR

Disbelief characterized the reaction in America to the breakup of the Soviet Union. (Ronald Reagan had predicted that communism would fail, but most assumed his forecasting was merely wishful thinking.) Gorbachev's actions after he assumed power took the world by surprise, and the Soviet Union's breakup that followed apparently was unforeseen by all, including Gorbachev.

During the Cold War, U.S. military defense leadership felt it necessary to rate as serious the possibility that the USSR might invade Western Europe. The rationale behind the NATO and the U.S. defense budgets was tied to this prediction. More recently, declassified papers from the ex-communist states of Eastern Europe have disclosed the forecasting of the Soviet Union during that same period. Amazingly, the USSR, it is now known, based most of its military planning on its prediction that the "aggressive capitalistic" NATO states, led by America, might attempt to take control of Eastern Europe.

THE BREADTH OF WRONG PREDICTIONS

Importantly bad prediction activity continues unabated. A day
and a half before the horrible Hurricane Charley hit Florida on
August 13, 2004, the National Oceanic and Atmospheric
Administration (NOAA) predicted that it would be a Category 2
storm, "shy of major hurricane status" and with maximum winds
of 177 kilometers per hour. The storm made landfall as a
Category 4 with winds at 241 kilometers per hour that killed people and left billions of dollars in damages.

In its September 19, 2005, issue, *Fortune* magazine admitted
that it had not been totally reliable in its published prophesying.
Fortune cited the following of its prediction boo-boos:

> *July 1934.* "Fascism remains, like the tariff, essentially a
> local issue."
>
> *March 1939.* "It appears practically impossible for Roosevelt
> to be reelected in 1940 unless his opposition is seriously
> divided between the Republicans and a third party."
>
> *February 1954.* "In several important respects the stock mar-
> ket appears to have become obsolete."
>
> *July 1972.* "The rotary engine has emerged almost abruptly
> as the coming prime source of automotive power in the U.S.,
> if not in the world."
>
> *February 1974.* "Climatologists now blame those recurring
> droughts and floods on a global cooling trend."
>
> *December 1974.* "Zero population growth [in the United States]
> is no longer a far-fetched notion but a real possibility."

November 1976. "The Last Billionaires: We may never see their like again."

January 30, 1978. "Fusion power—safe, clean, and virtually inexhaustible—is envisioned toward the end of the century."

June 2, 1980. "Comeback Decade for the American Car"

July 28, 1980. "Ronald Reagan won't beat Jimmy Carter." [The Gipper won in a landslide.]

June 12, 1995. "Get Ready for the Flat Tax; It's Hot, It's Now, It Could Change the Way you Live."

ECONOMICS FORECASTS

No effort at predicting is more vigorous than that devoted to the economy. No predicting pursuit has assembled more outstanding brainpower. And it is notorious for producing inaccurate forecasts that are nevertheless influential.

The planning of budgets, investments, marketing, expansions, terminations, and virtually every other aspect of the operation of business and government is always accomplished with consideration of inflation as it is and is estimated to become in the period ahead. This is despite errors in predicting inflation rates that run around 40 percent when made six months ahead of the year being forecast and 30 percent at the start of that year. Federal experts estimate the U.S. economic growth a year ahead and miss it regularly by at least 25 percent.[12]

Alan Greenspan, the former chairman of the Federal Reserve, speaking to Congress about the forecasts he had earlier given them of coming national surpluses, said, "It turns out we were all wrong."

How can we avoid being so often badly wrong and accomplish intelligent forecasting instead?

In the field of economics, no better example exists of past failure to constantly probe future possibilities, and then act so as to better shape the future, than does the global chaos in the financial world in late 2008. As this book is being written, both government and private entities are engaged in desperate efforts to avert collapse as stock markets plummet and bankruptcies rise. (This is further discussed in Chapter 3.)

Some predicting of the financial "black hole" did take place, but hardly at all by those in government and private entities with the power and authority to prevent the housing bubble and its burst and the credit availability's plunge.[13] With recession now judged a certainty and its cure uncertain, possibilities for the future are now receiving broad attention with regard to predictions.[14]

Chapter Two | Near-Term Forecasting

In discussing procedures for making useful predictions, it often will be helpful to consider such efforts in two separate categories: near-term and long-term forecasting. Near-term forecasting is exemplified by the regular quarter-year reporting of operating results by America's publicly owned corporations and the accompanying forecasts issued by their top managements of expected performance in a short period ahead. Much of business activity is covered by such reports and forecasts. The accuracy of the forecasts will depend to a large extent on the soundness of an organization's short-term record keeping, reporting, and forecasting.

This book's emphasis is on long-term predicting, particularly by business organizations. There are important differences between short-term and long-term predicting, but there are also similarities. A business unit that does not produce competent short-term forecasting of its operating results is likely to fall short also in long-term forecasting. Moreover, some bad habits or the indifference of business managers that cause failures to perceive what might happen in the very near future will likely also handicap those managers in their attempts to envisage problems and opportunities in the period further ahead. In this chapter we shall give emphasis to some principles that should guide short-term forecasting.

Managers of businesses arrange to receive detailed monthly accounting figures describing the status of the company—its revenues, shipments, work in process, cash flow, capital expenditures, net earnings, sales backlogs, and so on—which are continually under computerized preparation. Also, guidance as to quarterly results and forecasts for a year or so into the future are steadily provided to the public. The quarterly forecasts usually turn out to be inaccurate but not severely so. Deviations of the actual realizations from what had been anticipated are only infrequently so bad as to impair the value of the forecasting as a tool for good internal management and for professional outsiders to assess the business results reasonably well. Government regulating and taxing agencies, shareholders, professional securities analysts, the business news media, and others expect to have available up-to-date accounting and forecast data at least each yearly quarter on all publicly held corporations. Creating, issuing, and studying these quarterly reports constitute a substantial fraction of the work efforts of well over a million U.S. business and government employees.

The other category, long-term forecasting, is broader. It consists of prognostications of the future workings and developments of the entity concerned and of the changing social-economic-political-technological factors that influence its future. Unlike the short-term quarterly report forecasting of the first category, with detailed accounting data as its foundation, the long-term prediction category has to include numerous interacting characteristics of the world's activities that are difficult to measure. Moreover, the relationships among its interacting parameters are not usually clearly understood.

As an example in the first category, short-term forecasting, the amount of a factory's work in process for the present quarter tells something rather highly connected about the probable value of the goods-shipped figure for following quarters. In turn, those figures help to forecast the cash that will be received from customers for the quarters after that. In contrast, long-term figures such as interest, inflation, foreign exchange rates, trade balances, and many other international economic indicators cannot be predicted confidently even for a few months ahead, still less for years from now, even when those figures may be known accurately today. A single country's economy has so many dimensions and categories that it is impossible to fully document and analyze each one so that highly accurate long-term predicting can be accomplished. Many influential factors are not even measured and recorded. Try to predict NASA's budget five years from now, or the price of oil then, or the Federal Reserve's interest rates, or the stock market a year (or even a month) ahead. On the day Hitler became dictator of Germany, no predictor could know the date of his potentially invading other nations, even if it were thought he surely would attempt doing so.

The two categories of prediction, short term and long term, are different as to what management benefit might be derived from the forecast effort. Also varying between the two categories are the criteria for judging the success of attempts at prediction. For example, how high must a miss be before the attempt to predict is worthless? Even the way the foretelling effort should best be mounted is not always the same for the two categories.

THE PREDICTING-PLANNING PARTNERSHIP

We have asserted that the predicting activity of leadership can be valuable even with results far from perfect because it can lead to steps taken in time to shape the future to be better than it might have been otherwise. To elucidate further the potential usefulness of such forecasting, we must associate it with another essential activity of managers, namely, planning. As to good predicting and good planning, "you can't have one without the other," as the popular song goes. How useful indeed can your forecast be to you without a coordinated plan to realize that forecast's picture of the period ahead if the forecast appears beneficial or without a determined scheme to alter the future if it looks bad? Conversely, why should you have confidence that your plan is sensible when you have not assessed and predicted whether the plan will be realized? If you did do that analysis, then in effect you will have made a forecast.

But planning and predicting, closely related and necessary as both these management functions may be, are not identical in their objectives. Consider a football analogy. A quarterback calls a particular play. That is the plan for the team for the next dozen seconds. But it is a hope, not a prediction, that the play will go as planned. Maybe when the play was designed, it was estimated that it would be achieved about every other time, and that was deemed a good enough performance. Perhaps the plan included an attempted forward pass that, if completed, might result in a touchdown; but if only a first down should be achieved, such deviation from a more ambitious plan would still be rated satisfactory. Creating both a forecast and a plan should add to the value of each.

A leader of a business may put into effect a plan to increase reported earnings by a high percentage in the next year, with promised rewards for key employees if they actually realize it. Whether it is reached may depend on many diverse issues, like the past success record of the team members and hence their confidence. The manager may believe that the accomplishments will be superior to the result likely to occur if a less ambitious goal were set. The manager's own confidential prediction may be that the actual performance will be well below the plan. In other words, that leader may purposely announce a plan that differs from his or her own prediction. The manager may deliberately push the plan knowing that it is optimistic, ambitious, and hard driven in order to elicit more intense effort by the organization, or to stimulate innovation, or to challenge or aid himself or herself in rating members of the management team, or to uncover limitations on the organization's basic abilities, or to accomplish other objectives.

All in all, good planning is essential to good forecasting and vice versa. Both functions are often carried out by the same people in an organization. Equally often, however, especially in very large businesses or government organizations, the two functions are carried out in different parts of the organization that are not always in strong communication and consultation with each other. That is not necessarily harmful. The forecasting might be short range, like the production of quarterly performance reports with accompanying future earnings guidance. Others in the organization, working separately, might concentrate on creating plans for the longer term. They will ponder strategy for growth and perform studies on how to improve performance. They will consider alternatives and assess risk-to-return ratios for competitive plans. This separation of planning and forecasting sometimes can be advantageous for improving focus, efficiency, and clarity for each function. Still, if each of the two activities is carried on in too much isolation from the other, then neither the planning nor the predicting, be it short or long range, will be of maximum aid in the overall management of the organization.

THE QUARTERLY REPORT

Competent management of any activity includes, of course, much analysis of the immediate past and present status of the operation. Even if regular and frequent disclosure of this information were not required by outside rule setters, such as the federal government's Securities and Exchange Commission (SEC), the managers of the activities need it. This applies not only to publicly held corporations but to all businesses—in fact, to all managed entities, be they foundations, hospitals, churches, government units, universities, professional athletic teams, or accounting firms. The managers must know what happened in the most recent period to the balance sheet of assets and liabilities. Did liabilities expand? Was debt reduced? Did the cash on hand grow or drop? How big were revenues and various expenses? How much profit was earned?

As the manager, you likely will have called earlier for forecasts of actual accounting figures. Did the actual figures turn out to be close to what it was estimated they would be? If the amount of cash on hand had been forecast by you to be too low, you would have borrowed more, or cut expenditures previously planned, or done something else to ensure the availability of sufficient cash. Parts produced in a manufacturing company in an earlier month and that are now in inventory should show up in products and assembled and sold in following months. Each piece of present accounting data should have led you to a later figure sensibly forecasted for a future date. Existing data together with knowledge of the relationships—between data for the immediate past and present and those describing the near-term future—are fundamental to the forecasting process. That is the basic characteristic of the short-term forecasting category.

How important is it to a manager that the monthly forecasting be accurate? Every public corporation's judges are of many different kinds: shareholders, the business reporting media, banks and other financial entities with whom the corporation deals, customers, employees and their unions, management personnel, contractors, the federal regulatory bodies, even the U.S. Congress and the Department of Justice on occasion—the list is long, and the separate observers differ as to which aspects of the corporation's performance interests them most. The judges vary greatly also in their competence to judge. In any case, the reactions of these many constituencies to the quarterly reports and to the accompanying short-term forecast indications by management can affect the market price of the shares, the confidence in the company of potential customers, the morale and stability of the employees, and, overall, the success of management.

HONEST FORECASTING

In view of these factors it should not be surprising that forecasters often forecast low to outsiders because they can thus cause quarterly reports of actual results to exceed, or at least meet, the results those judgers have earlier been led to expect. Managers and forecasters generally please critics when they perform better than promised. Now, it so happens that the internal forecasting procedure in any large company—in fact, even for many small ones—involves integrating the separate forecasts of the necessarily separately managed segments of the whole. Each segment manager submits a forecast to a higher-up who assembles the overall forecast. If every segment manager knows that the next higher boss is certain to be very unhappy, maybe even severely unpleasant, when the segment manager misses her or his forecast, that lower manager can be expected to habitually forecast low to play it safe. If this practice goes all the way to the top, the company's results may usually exceed the forecasts.

But that means the CEO will not honestly have described to the outside world what the company truly expects, and the company, described so pessimistically, might be rated lower than it deserves to be. When a business quarterly report beats the expected performance, that welcome announcement may cause the stock price to rise temporarily. But eventually, steady, inaccurate forecasting will lower confidence in the management's understanding of what it is managing, and that is certainly not good.

Perhaps the rule for a competent and respected forecaster should be simply to engage in honest forecasting. But honest forecasters of short-term results can still miss their forecasts badly, even if only a month has passed. Some customers may fail to make payments as expected. Output may have been delayed because of a sudden quality control problem or an unanticipated union issue in the factory. A supplier may fail to ship on time. An unforeseen litigation expense might arise. An unexpected product recall might be required. To be honest does not necessarily equate to forecasting accurately. Honesty may be essential but it is not sufficient.

POOR REPORTING AND FORECASTING

If short-term forecasts and actuals are persistently and greatly mismatched, that may be because the forecasting is poorly done. The accuracy of forecasting a company's results depends largely on having readily available the data on what has occurred in the recent past and what the situation appears to be in the present. The ability to predict the future is bound to be handicapped if pertinent facts are missing, in error, or incomplete. If your forecasts seem too often to be too wrong, you should look first to see if, when you made your predictions, your data-producing function let you down.

Some short-term forecasting that deserves a poor grade is merely the result of sloppy last-minute efforts. The sector manager may be swamped with priority problems and opportunities and may be waiting until the last day of the month to start turning out the required forecast, finishing in a mad rush minutes before the deadline. Higher-level managers can fail to notice such bad habits and not act to eliminate them—perhaps because they also are guilty of engaging in hazardous scheduling of their time.

It can be worse. Your problems as a manager may be well beyond your bad forecasting per se. Your poor predictions may result from your not having gotten your management act together. Perhaps you do not know and understand, or are not adequately in control of, the activity in your charge. In any case, you should be greatly interested in learning why your short-term forecasting is unacceptably inaccurate. The management level above you should be interested in learning this about you, too, and providing guidance as necessary.

DISCRETIONARY ACCOUNTING

A business corporation's management, before the establishment of the Fair Disclosure Regulation (Reg FD) in 2000 and Sarbanes-Oxley (SOX) in 2002, used to be allowed considerable discretion, legally and ethically, in the treatment of many items that comprise forecasts of both the balance sheet (of assets and liabilities) and the profit and loss (P&L) statement.[1] Accuracy had not always been the sole consideration in forecasting operating results for a quarter or more ahead. To an accepted extent before the passage of SOX, whether a forecast was going to be missed, met, or exceeded was adjustable by management, with changes often made just before the public announcements. Discretion is still allowed, but companies are now much more restricted in the way they must communicate forward-looking information. We illustrate by example.

Suppose a company has acquired a patent for $25 million. The patent was purchased in the belief that the profit generated in exploiting that patent would greatly exceed the purchase price. But suppose some other firm suddenly announces it holds an earlier patent superseding the first company's purchased patent, making it worthless. Suppose also that an initial examination does not make clear whether the outside claim has merit. Instead, it looks as though a long investigation and even litigation may be required.

How should the company handle the disclosure of this situation? Should it announce a $25 million loss? If it does this, some shareholders will sell their falling stock. But what if the purchased patent is later upheld, a great profit stream results, and the stock soars? Might not those who sold low and missed the rise have a basis for suing the management for misleading them by a wrong announcement? Could they not claim the company leaders "should have known" the outside claim was without merit and the patent good?

Conversely, what if the company delays making a public announcement and then has to disclose a $25 million loss years later when it becomes certain the purchased patent is of no value and the stock then falls? Might not those shareholders who bought stock earlier sue because they would not have purchased shares had they known?

This kind of judgment call can be expected to happen time and again in a large company. General accounting rules and advice solicited from accountants and lawyers will sometimes appear to settle whether losses and earnings should be recorded quickly or delayed—that is, whether specific items should be conservatively or optimistically defined. Sometimes, however, the company management will be forced to make the judgment as to whether its investment will be recovered or not—that is, it will be forced to give its view of the most probable outcome. The accounting rules would require management to accompany the reported financial results with adequately detailed explanations. If the write-off of the $25 million is taken early and a subsequent court ruling is favorable, the company would be able to book greater future earnings as a result. However, if these future earnings are material, then the reason for these higher future earnings would need to be disclosed by management. Stockholders should not be misled into thinking the company's earnings for that future reported period have risen because the management has performed brilliantly!

Another example will be helpful. An earthquake damages a company's facility, halting production and delaying shipments, and this lowers associated earnings. Insurance covers the loss totally, the company's legal advisors state. The insurance company differs, saying most of the losses are not covered. It will take over a year to settle the matter; it may require a court battle. Should the debated amount be listed as owed to the company even though it is to be paid later by the insurer, as the attorneys claim should occur? Or should it be taken as a loss to the extent the insurance company says it is not obligated ever to pay it? Again, now with current, more stringent accounting rules in effect, management can record expected recoveries from the insurer only if those recoveries are deemed probable. Management's judgments must be completely documented. Any deviation, manipulation, or misrepresentation, thanks to SOX, will be subject to severe penalties (perhaps even including jail sentences).

In opening this chapter, we stated that, although the main thrust of this book is how to accomplish useful long-term predicting, it was sensible first to discuss near-term forecasting. This is because if near-term efforts are poorly performed, then it is likely that some of the reasons for the unsatisfactory results will carry over into attempts at making long-range forecasts. In closing this chapter—with the rest of this text now devoted to long-term predicting—it is sensible also to point out that many of the procedures we shall next present for achieving useful long-term predictions will apply as well to improving short-term forecasting.

Chapter Three | Possibilities, Then Predictions: The Four- Measures Procedure

Let us suppose that you, a management leader, are engaged in what you hope will be intelligent forecasting. Your aim is to spot major developments in the future and then to act early so as to shape that future. But this does not mean you should rush to paint a picture of the period ahead. Something else should come first. You should assemble possibilities. For that process, you must be generously inclusive. You should seek a broad perception of conceivable—and perhaps sometimes even seemingly rather improbable—coming happenings.

When predictors miss badly, when they have failed to foresee important occurrences, it is often because their consideration of future possibilities was too limited. Their imaginations and compilations failed to encompass an adequate spectrum of coming events that, were they to occur, would present either severely negative challenges that the forecasters then would regret not having prepared for or attractive opportunities they did not anticipate, so failed to grasp.[1]

As you contemplate future possibilities, you must be bold, your inhibitions curbed. For one thing, you must force yourself to imagine what awfully bad things might happen. Be a worrywart, a severe pessimist. Could a competitor surprise you with a superior product or shock you by greatly lowering prices? Could a key sponsor abandon your project? Might an essential member of your team quit with no notice? Could the economy, especially as it might pertain to your activity, take an unexpectedly bad turn? Might we even enter into a long period of worldwide economic chaos and severe recession? Might a competitor's radically new invention cause your product to be suddenly out-of-date? Might Congress pass a bill ruling out what you thought would be a favorable tax deduction? Might terrorism worsen greatly and particularly affect the operations under your responsibility?

Also, of course, you must indulge in thinking exceedingly optimistically. Might an unlikely new event lead to an unplanned-for advantageous twist for the future of your activity? What could it be? A new wonderful marketing idea? A scientific discovery or technology breakthrough in your own research lab? A tough competitor going out of business? A great candidate for acquisition popping up suddenly?

Broaden the scope of your imaginings to include a plethora of big external forces that, if they happened, would require major changes in your future plans—for example, a war breaking out, a stock market collapse, an inflation surge, a spreading pernicious computer virus, a bad natural phenomenon surfacing to worsen life on Earth, a truly dramatic increase in the cost of energy, or a new and strongly financed foreign-based company suddenly entering your field as a determined competitor. Be loose, not fussy, as you assemble possibilities. Allow yourself to enjoy a bit of near absurdity resulting from the fact that the probabilities are so tiny that some conceivable developments you include will happen. You should not worry about the little chance of actual occurrence as you force yourself to concoct a mélange of possibilities. You can eliminate the worthless candidates later, when you shift from assembling mere possibilities to focusing and deciding on actionable predictions. Pondering some overly fanciful possibilities might surprise you by stimulating you to identify reasons why they are not so unlikely to occur as you first might have thought.

Compiling useful possibilities is not the same as uncovering fascinating possibilities. Some outlandish and indefensible future events can be enticingly attractive, especially to habitually happy optimists. Setting down terribly sad possibilities may be just as entrancing to severe pessimists. The weaker the predictor's requirement that strong rationales should exist for including specific possibilities, the easier, of course, will be the formulation of them. An intelligent forecaster will not include a possibility simply because it is preferred and the forecaster hopes it will occur. A possibility must feel right to a cold, calculating lister.

It must be granted that a danger exists of your taking too seriously your nominated possibilities. Perhaps very different and much more important events from those you will have listed will occur instead. It is necessary that you guard against being wholly unprepared for the actualities when they arrive because of a preoccupation with preparing for possibilities that never happen. It is wise always to remember that your enumerated future developments are merely possibilities, so the intelligent approach is never to commit irrevocably and exclusively to them. Instead, the described potential future events should be continually reconsidered. The inventory of possibilities should be edited and updated, items added or deleted, as time passes. As a final insurance, one possibility (perhaps half seriously and half facetiously suggested here) should be placed at the very top of the compendium—namely, the possibility that all the listings that follow will turn out to be wrong.

THE FOUR-MEASURES RATING

Let us now imagine that you, a would-be intelligent predictor, have assembled a list of possibilities for the future by combining wisdom gained from experience with uninhibited imagination. What you now desire is to produce specific predictions that might lead you to early action to maximize potential benefits from future events and minimize detriments those occurrences might bring. To achieve this, we recommend you assign four ratings to each tabulated possibility:

A. *Probability.* What is the likelihood that the possibility actually will occur, ranging perhaps from almost certain to extremely unlikely?

B. *Timing.* If the possibility occurs, when might that be—soon or far off in time?

C. *Impact.* If the possibility should actually occur, how relevant would that be to your specific interests? Would the resulting opportunities or penalties be great or only minor?

D. *Action potential.* Assuming the prediction proves accurate, how practical is it for you to act now so as to shape the future and cause it to turn out better?

A possibility deserving priority attention would be one that appeared highly probable to come about, that would soon be very disadvantageous or would offer great advantages if it did, and, finally, that allowed for much to be done ahead of time to accentuate the positives and diminish the negatives. In contrast, a possibility extreme the other way would merit less attention if it described a future development that had a low probability of happening, that appeared far off should it occur, that would exert only a minor effect in your particular arena, and that allowed for little to be done by you ahead of time to shape and improve the future.

It usually will be smart for you to assign numbers (1 to 10) to these four ratings (A, B, C, and D) and then add the scores. Those possibilities scoring nearest to 40 would be favored to receive further analysis. Even when these numeric ratings cannot be considered adequate measurements—because everything worth predicting has unmeasurable aspects—this quantitative scoring serves as a first step and as a guide as you go on to probe the important nonnumeric, qualitative characteristics of the possibility. The numeric score should not be the last word in rating a possibility. But if that score is very low, then you must ask yourself why you would contemplate elevating that possibility to a

prediction and start detailed actions. And if the numeric rating
is very high, you must equally strive to understand why you do
not immediately elevate that possibility to a prediction and proceed accordingly.

A HALF-CENTURY-OLD EXAMPLE

We recommend the above described Four-Measures procedure to
rate future possibilities when they are being analyzed for inclusion as predictions because of our success in our past use of this
approach. (One of the authors has used the essence of this procedure for over six decades.) We illustrate this with further com-
ments on the failure to predict and act upon the coming of the
"Space Age." We already touched on this topic in Chapter 1 in
the context of the failure of the U.S. government and industry to
anticipate the Soviet Union's launching of its *Sputnik* satellite.
In particular, we called attention to the fact that only one
American company acted early in anticipation of a space race
with the USSR and of the developing of a multidimensional effort
by the United States in the military, commercial, and research
applications of space technology.

TRW Inc. was that company. Based on its predictions, it created a new corporation named Space Technology Laboratories a
year before the *Sputnik* launch.[2] The arrival of the space field
had been judged a strong possibility by TRW substantially earlier. TRW was not explicitly using the Four-Measures approach
in the 1950s, but its elements were in the minds of TRW's leadership. A retro-look at this time of the likely scoring had the
approach been applied then may be interesting. The probability

of the space field developing would have been rated very high. We would now say that possibility A was seen to merit a 10. The coming of spacecraft was considered only a mere few years away at that time because the ICBM development had successfully reached the full-scale stage—launchings at several thousand miles distance with high accuracy in landing. So TRW, in effect, would have rated possibility B a 9. The ICBM program that TRW then had the responsibility for leading caused that company to be heavily involved in developing the technology basic to utilizing space. Consequently, TRW, as a business corporation, naturally assigned a high priority to exploiting to the maximum its acquired technological expertise. The impact on TRW would thus also have been rated extremely high. By today's quantitative measure, C would have been seen then to be a 10.

Did TRW possess the ability to act on this space potential ahead of the era's arrival, this being the fourth measure, D? Yes. D would have deserved a rating of 10 if TRW were willing to take the risk of making a rather huge investment. If so, then the resulting Four-Measures score would have been:

A. Probability	10
B. Timing	9
C. Impact	10
D. Action potential	10
Total	39

That risk was in fact taken. A hundred-acre plot of land was acquired to house the unique facilities required for the development, construction, and testing of spacecraft components and complete spacecrafts. The manufacture of every tiny part and the assembly of an entire spacecraft, it was clear, would have to be accomplished with extreme care and ascertained to be correct, ready, and of adequate life expectancy. (After a launch into space discloses flaws in a spacecraft, it is not exactly practical to bring it down temporarily for repair or to visit it in space and modify it.) All would have to be subjected to simulation of the conditions during a launch and in the space environment. To provide for such unprecedented testing, it would be necessary to devise and create "first-time" new testing apparatus and chambers.

The prediction of the arrival of the new space technology field had to include, of course, some scenarios as to how the U.S. government would come to see and act on such a development. TRW predicted, for instance, that, in addition to assigning military space projects to the U.S. Air Force (USAF), the government would also need to create a new government entity to manage some of its space-related activities—which the government did in creating NASA. TRW predicted that the new agency would be offering exciting nonmilitary contracts—just as after World War II the Atomic Energy Commission (AEC) was formed to ensure proper attention to the development and use of nuclear technology for civilian purposes.

This risk taking, based on attempting intelligent forecasting, proved successful. During the 50 years since the *Sputnik* launch, TRW—now Northrop Grumman—has been a leader in developing and applying space technology, and it has also been a profitable business unit with cumulative space revenues that have passed the $100 billion level since its founding.

A MORE RECENT EXAMPLE

The technique of forecasting that first lists possibilities and then employs the Four-Measures ratings to progress from possibilities to predictions, often works well. It can be simple, logical, and quick. But at times the situation is too complex for so straight-forward a procedure. Even then, however, the approach usually remains useful, but it serves more as a guide that steers and points. We next discuss such an example.

As this book is being written, the U.S. Air Force is conduct-ing a competition to determine which of two bidders, Northrop Grumman or Boeing, will be awarded a huge military procure-ment contract (expected to grow to around $35 billion over the next decade). The project encompasses a new fleet of aerial refu-eling tankers to enable the employment of U.S. air power any-where in the world where the nation's security requires it. Air Force officials have designated this tanker program as the high-est in weapons-buying priority.

Because of the size of this program and its importance to national security, this competition has been receiving unusual attention from many sources. The larger the number of involved participants and the greater their influences, the broader becomes the spread of possibilities that require consideration. The main large contractors, the host of smaller but important sub-contractors, members of Congress pressing for awards to suppli-ers in their states and districts, and the media—all are in the act. Politics intertwines with national security in ways enormously difficult to predict. The impact of winning or losing the contract competition on the industry teams involved will be enormous, of course, as will be the impact of the award on the economic health of the regions where those companies are situated. Forecasters attempting to predict how the tanker competition will end will need to create possibility lists as huge as the number of billions of dollars involved.

For the management of Northrop Grumman, the key possibility to ponder initially was whether its chance of winning would be high enough to justify allocating the necessary financial resources and the efforts of a large team of its most outstanding engineers that alternatively might be employed on other projects. Filling the Air Force's tanker needs with the highest performance and at the lowest cost involved the careful selecting of the airplane itself, its engines, the apparatus for transfer of the fuel from tanker to bombers and fighter craft, and an array of equipment for control, navigation, communication, and self-protection. Study by Northrop's engineers of the availability of suitably large commercial aircraft made it clear that only Boeing and EADS's Airbus subsidiary could possibly provide aircraft candidates for consideration. Northrop's analysts found themselves concluding that an existing EADS plane would be superior to any Boeing plane for the Air Force's announced requirements for the tankers as to the quantity of fuel carried, available space for passengers and freight, costs, and potential for on-time delivery.[3]

EADS was anxious to team with Northrop Grumman for this competition, as was General Electric to supply the engines. A possibility deserving a high probability of occurrence was that some politicians might be prejudiced against the participation of EADS because that company is based in Europe. The criticism would especially not be surprising from those senators or representatives whose areas happen to house company facilities that would lose out if the Northrop-EADS team won. Now, it happens that the U.S. Defense Department (DoD) implemented years ago the practice of obtaining designs and manufactured parts from companies headquartered in the NATO countries and other friendly nations (for example, Australia and Israel). The U.S. Congress passed legislation making this international sourcing legal and proper, this to ensure the DoD's filling its needs at minimum cost and encouraging military cooperation with its closest allies.[4] In the past in accordance with accepted practices, the U.S. military has purchased bombs from France, helicopter equipment from Italy, and aircraft engines from Britain. The United States, however, is the leader by far in export of military gear, this constituting a very substantial part of U.S. exports. U.S. allies purchase many times more military equipment from America than America purchases from them. (Parts being made in one country for assembly in another is particularly common for civilian airplanes, each company needing to look for quality parts at the lowest cost.)[5]

The plan to meet head-on this "foreign source" negative possibility was for EADS to become an American as well as a European company with regard to airplane production. The Northrop-EADS team boldly proposed that two new plants would be built in the U.S. state of Alabama—one in which the proven EADS commercial airplane would be assembled and the other in which Northrop Grumman would add to and modify the plane to make it a militarized tanker. (Moreover, EADS planned also to assemble in its new Alabama facility its freight-carrying commercial planes.) If the contract were won by Northrop Grumman, the number of new jobs created in the United States was estimated at 48,000.[6]

Northrop concluded that the probability of its winning the competition was high enough to justify bidding against Boeing for this tanker contract. Indeed, the U.S. Air Force announced that Northrop had been selected to receive the contract. Then, to illustrate the complexity of forecasting for the future in this instance, the losing bidder, Boeing, delivered a formal protest to the Congress (specifically to the Government Accountability Office [GAO]), as losing bidders are privileged to do regarding DoD competitions. The GAO, citing some procedural flaws, concluded that the Air Force had not processed the competition as it should have. The DoD responded that it would reconsider the competitive proposals.

Consider now a few of the possibilities that had to be pondered by a forecaster at this point in the history of the tanker procurement:

- The DoD might announce that after further consideration it would adhere to its original decision to award the contract to Northrop.
- The DoD might award the contract to Boeing.
- The DoD might reformulate its request for proposals to significantly alter the kind of airplane required, thereby sending the competition back to square 1.
- The DoD might decide to divide the tanker procurement between Northrop and Boeing, stating that upon further study it was concluded that continued competition between the two sources would lead to cost reductions and improved performance sufficient to compensate for the added costs of maintaining two different tanker capabilities.

- The delay might cause the final decision to be funded in the next presidential and congressional term when changes could be great. The national budget for defense, and even overall policy regarding national security, might go through major changes. This could conceivably affect even the priority of the tanker program.
- The prospect of successive protests, delays, and congressional blocking actions might create the most unfortunate possible outcome—that a new tanker might never be built at all.[7]

We shall not attempt here to predict the future of the tanker program. The foregoing has been presented to illustrate that complex situations can be probed advantageously, although not always settled, by the Four-Measures approach. By the time the reader has arrived at this page that future may have become clear.

THE WORLDWIDE ECONOMIC CRISIS OF 2008

Imagine that leaders of the U.S. Treasury, the Federal Reserve, Wall Street, and the banks and other financial institutions worldwide were all accustomed to using the Four-Measures approach in their forecasting. Their regularly listed future possibilities then would of course have included the optimistic one: continuing ready availability of credit, rising housing prices and stock markets, high debt-leveraging as a route to high returns on investments—all persisting for the long-term future. But any management group applying the Four-Measures approach also surely would have felt it necessary to include another and pessimistic possibility. They would have considered a coming credit crunch, the bursting of the home price bubble, a stock market crash, a flood of bankruptcies, perhaps even worldwide panic and the start of a very bad recession.

Suppose this economic chaos possibility had been rated by the Four-Measures approach a few years ago. What probability, "A," of its occurring would have been chosen? Would it not have been set high when considered against past bubble bursts and sudden bear markets in the American and world economies? Surely the number for "A" would have been 8, 9, or maybe even 10. What about the next measure, "B," about whether it might come soon or later? Again—with evidence surfacing of rising defaults on mortgage payments (by the many home buyers whose interest payments were high relative to their incomes), the Four Measures would have favored "soon" with the score for "B" also being close to 10. Would the occurrence materially affect the forecaster's organization should the possibility actually come to pass, "C"? Yes, it certainly might, perhaps drastically—another score of 9 or 10. A forecaster employed by any company operating with a high debt-to-equity ratio would know that to wait might be very dangerous because paying down debt after panic conceivably sets in might be virtually impossible.

Finally, could the business entity's management do something effective early, "D," to shape the future, making it substantially better? Of course. Stock could be issued at a good price to increase equity and pay off debt, and those assets whose market value might have been anticipated as likely to drop greatly could have been sold early.

In our hypothetical example, the total Four-Measures score for the pessimistic possibility would have been in the high 30s, therefore worthy of serious consideration. Accordingly, those accustomed to carefully applying the Four-Measures approach in their forecasting would have been more sensitive to leading indicators, and might more likely have chosen to act early rather than to take the risk of enormous loss were they to make the sole prediction that the world economy would continue to thrive.

PREDICTIONS OFTEN WRONG

What about those other possibilities of lower Four-Measures ratings where it is not as clear how deserving such possibilities might be of further effort? As to these, we first must keep in mind that predictions often turn out wrong. Before setting aside a possibility that scores low numerically and thus initially seems to warrant little attention, it should be examined further in at least one important respect. Even if it rates only a very low probability of occurring and appears very far off in time, what if it nevertheless also is judged to exert an enormous effect should it occur? To a predictor it would not be intelligent forecasting to set that possibility aside easily. What if it turned out to be wrong to have rated it unlikely? What if it really *were* to happen, and soon? What would you do?

Did the managements of Ford and General Motors seriously consider 10 years ago that their annual losses would ever be so great as to cause the business media within a decade to be writing dramatically about the possibility of their companies' going bankrupt?

If the mayor of Peachtree City, Georgia, in 1995 made some notes about his city's likely status 10 years into the future, he was probably very optimistic. Peachtree's 35,000 residents then were enjoying a well above average American life in a city judged one of the nation's best—good schools, essentially no crime, beautiful golf courses, a haven for many airline pilots, an average household income close to $100,000, and a location convenient to Atlanta. But Peachtree was and is essentially a company town, and the company is Delta Airlines. It would not be amazing if the mayor's long-term prediction in 1995 failed to include as a possibility Delta's future bankruptcy even though he knew half of the residents of Peachtree were dependent on Delta's financial health.

WHY POSSIBILITIES ARE OFTEN MISSED

When forecasts have turned out wrong, it has often been because important possibilities for the future seemed too remote for their occurrences to be considered. Equally often the forecasters have lacked the amount of know-how, imagination, and curiosity necessary to perceive how the future might unfold. Of course, it is too much to expect even the most professionally qualified prognosticators to catch every significant change from present to future if it has hardly begun to form. But certain tendencies and patterns of operation that cause poor prediction scores are sometimes deeply ingrained in the predictors' makeups and cultures. Consequently, more intelligent prediction can be attained by excising bad habits. We cite some here:

- *Misused extrapolation.* The easiest prediction to make is that the present will continue into the long-range future largely unchanged. Some forecasters will be inclined to do this to excess for many reasons including:

- *Mental laziness.* Extrapolating often provides a forecast with the least effort. When earlier predictions based on no significant change have turned out correct, it is especially tempting to forecast the continuation of the present.

- *Inadequate competence.* If the predictor is ignorant of many important potential developments, the prediction of no new development is not unusual. If the predictor also lacks the analytical ability required to assess possibilities of change, a prediction of no important change is not surprising.

- *Too rushed for time.* Accomplishing careful prediction takes time. Predicting a continuation of the present doesn't.

- *Past success.* As we have had reason to note earlier, those successful for many years in a particular field are especially likely to possess only limited interest in predicting changes because they are so happy with the past and the present.

- *No competition.* Having no serious competitors is especially a handicap in long-term prognosticating. A near-monopoly supplier can easily become cocksure and arrogant, feeling little need for serious effort when predicting the future, it being so comforting to assume it will continue to be good.

- *The isolated predictor.* Often an important prediction chore is left to one person's judgment alone. Even for narrow areas of predicting (like the price a manufacturer forecasts for needed steel in the coming years), a second individual should check the figures. Two heads, assuming reasonable competence for each, are far better than one when the issue being predicted is heavily based on intuitive impressions (sometimes better called pure guesses) as distinct from facts. It is intelligent to debate differences of opinion even when one person alone will make the decision in the end. On major predictions, it is common that the final result will involve an assembly of many subpredictions by specialists each predicting a single piece. When a forecast has turned out to be mistaken, it can be seen at times that a single individual (one providing only a piece of the whole prediction) was so wrong and yet so influential as to ruin the overall accuracy. In the prediction game no key facet should be left to one predictor.

■ *Optimists and pessimists.* Prognosticating can be counted on to bring out the optimism of optimists and the pessimism of pessimists. It involves more than the trite "half-full" versus "half-empty" glass often used to compare optimists' and pessimists' diverse ways of thinking. If the leader of a business insistently demands "growth!" the managers below will give priority to optimistic possibilities, like large future rises in the growth of the entity. A common reason for wrong predictions, in other words, is a management culture that does not put realism first. The top executive pushes for optimistic forecasts and gets them, especially from optimists below. If the top is pessimistic, the forecasts from below will be pessimistic, especially from pessimists.

- *The champion predictor.* Some enjoy the experience of being amazingly prescient in their forecasting for a while with that excellent prediction performance well known. Such people are recognized as brilliant and visionary. Their reputations may indeed be deserved, stemming from a period of truly exceptional prediction performance. These individuals, however, are not equipped with magical prophesying powers. They must always employ substantial analytical and creative effort.

  Jack Welch, the famous outstanding past leader of General Electric, expanded that company's activities by steadily successful endeavors. He was a truly brilliant predictor. One day, GE added investment banking to its acquisition list hoping for the same impressive success as had been attained with previous additions. That turned out to be a mistake. We have to admire Welch, short and balding, when he blamed himself for the error saying, "I was on a roll. I didn't know diddly about that business. I thought I was six-feet-four with hair."

- *Understanding competitors.* If you are an intelligent predictor, you will always have in mind that it is not only your plans that count in determining your success but also the plans of your competitors. You naturally have a better understanding of your own activities than you do of your competitors' enterprises. A major reason for many wrong predictions is failure to allot sufficient effort to predicting the actions of competitors. Producers of television programs would experience fewer bad misses in their forecasting were they not faced with the difficult task of predicting how the public will react not only to theirs but to their competition's efforts to provide entertainment. We can say the same about producing autos, cell phones, or refrigerators, about managing hotels, and, of course, about leading governments. All too often an entity will expend substantial effort on making predictions for its own future activities but expend almost no effort on making predictions about its competitors activities. In such situations, prediction misses should be expected.

- *Lack of imagination.* It is not surprising that predictions are missed when to foresee coming occurrences requires the seers to be creative and original. If the prediction effort is important to an entity dominated by a need for innovation—such as the high-tech, advertising, and entertainment fields—then it is unwise to rely on unimaginative predictors. Their ideas are likely to be formed by a thinking process that characterizes the past but may not dominate in the future.

- *Lack of discipline.* Often poor predicting occurs simply because the forecasting effort is too casual, cavalier, unorganized, and/or unpolished—that is, it is done in a hit-or-miss and hurried style.

- *Ignoring the big picture.* In virtually all predictions about human endeavors, the future is influenced by unique factors, one of which is world events. As will be discussed in a later chapter, world events sometimes more than localized events can affect the future of a narrow piece of human activity. Forecasting misses will be lessened by appropriate consideration of the potential impact of those broader external influences. Doing at least a little thinking about the relationship of the broad to the narrow may cause some items to surface for further inquiry. That intelligent practice is not universal among predictors.

CONCLUSION

Competent management of every activity of our society must include attempts at envisaging the future, because it is not sufficient to react after the future unfolds. Although wholly accurate long-term prediction is impossible, useful forecasts—even if incomplete and often in error—are possible and mandatory. Steps must be taken ahead of time to maximize emerging opportunities and minimize the perceived negatives of coming developments—that is, to shape the future. To accomplish this in an intelligent way, we must continuously imagine possibilities for the period ahead and rate each possibility as to the following:

1. Probability of its occurrence
2. Timing of its occurrence
3. Its impact (for good or bad) on the predictor's activity
4. The capability to improve the future by taking action ahead of time

Predictors should give priority to those possibilities with the apparent highest total ratings. Predictors must recognize, however, that any prediction might well turn out to be wrong. Predictors accordingly should be prepared to alter plans when the future is seen to be developing in variance from the forecast.

The process of setting a final rating on a possibility can become complex. A particular possibility may appear to have a very low probability of ever happening, but the outcome, should the possibility come about, might be so consequential that planning absolutely must be carried out ahead of its possible arrival. See the following chart.

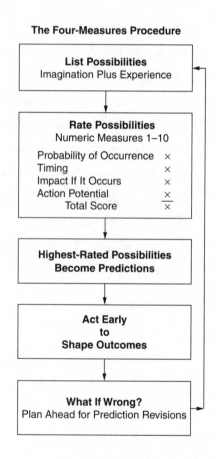

The Four-Measures Procedure

List Possibilities
Imagination Plus Experience

Rate Possibilities
Numeric Measures 1–10

Probability of Occurrence   ×
Timing   ×
Impact If It Occurs   ×
Action Potential   ×
Total Score   ×

Highest-Rated Possibilities
Become Predictions

Act Early
to
Shape Outcomes

What If Wrong?
Plan Ahead for Prediction Revisions

Chapter Four | Extrapolating from Past to Future

How can you best proceed to assemble a useful list of possibilities? We shall describe a number of practical ways. The first is to extrapolate. *Webster's* states that *extrapolation* is "the extending, inferring, or projecting of known data or experience from an observed past period so as to construct an image of a period ahead." Some things do not change greatly, some not quickly, some neither. The coming of electric lighting impaired the sale of kerosene lamps, and autos replaced horse buggies, but both changeovers took a while. Even when change is life altering, like the coming of TV, computers, cell phones, and the Internet, and the stock market crash of 2008, the future and the past usually share origins and characteristics, much like familial genes. Accordingly, it will make sense to list as possibilities careful extrapolations from the recent past. Extrapolation can be extremely useful, and in its more sophisticated embodiments, some of which we shall present in this chapter, it can involve many complexities in approach if the usefulness is to be fully realized.

Suppose you seek a quick estimate of future sales of one of the products of your company that has recorded nearly constant sales of that product in the last several years. Also, suppose that no reason is readily seen to expect the demand for that product to go up or down substantially. Then it is reasonable to consider, as one possibility, that the near-future years' annual revenues will be close to the recent past ones. This is a simple form of extrapolation, but it can be of value, even if only as a starting estimate. Extrapolation can be much more sophisticated and detailed, however, and often can be increasingly valuable as its more complex embodiments are employed.

EXTRAPOLATING RATES OF CHANGE

Imagine that your corporation was the leader last year in a certain product, enjoying 60 percent of the market, with the nearest contender's taking only 30 percent and the minor also-rans' taking only 10 percent. The most elementary of extrapolation would have you list the possibility that this ratio in market sharing will continue. Careful examination of the past, however, may cause you to rule out using the 60/30 figure as a realistic possibility even for the very next year. That is because you perceive that five years ago your company took 80 percent of the market and that same nearest competitor captured only 10 percent, an 80/10 ratio, one far more favorable than the immediate past year's 60/30. Moreover, you note you have increasingly lost sales to that competitor every year of the last five, the accumulated share loss over that period being the noted 20 percent. Extrapolation as a means of acquiring a list of realistic future possibilities, we readily realize from this example, should not be always a linear projection of only a single handy number that describes just one aspect of the past. The *rate of change* in a key figure may be the important item to extrapolate. Indeed, it even could be that an increasing rate of change of a principal number may be the factor most suitable to extrapolate.

To clarify, observe that the market share loss over the past five years averaged 4 percent per year. Might that 4 percent average annual drop be expected to continue? Not if the *rate* of loss in recent years has not been constant. The yearly market losses over the past five years, we imagine we discover, were specifically 1 percent the first year, 1.5 percent the next, then 2.5 percent, 5 percent, and 10 percent with the cumulative result at five years' end being that noted total of 20 percent. Observing these important figures, it is clear that the *rate* of loss of the market share of your product actually grew alarmingly, recently doubling each year. Thus your extrapolating, if it is to yield truly useful possibilities, might better postulate a continuation of this *increasing rate* of market share decrease. That means your competitor seems about to put you totally out of business! That catastrophe becomes, by extrapolation, the leading possibility!

Of course, we have pictured an extreme case. So great an increase in market share loss would get the management's attention early if the product were a major one for the company. It would not go unnoticed—which would be evidence of bad forecasting procedure—with no action taken for five years. But managers typically have many opportunities and problems arising on a daily basis and will not always be on top of every one. Not all such potentials can be expected to manifest themselves readily. Eventually extremely bad news will reach everyone, but management needs to become aware of dangers when they have only begun to form, when they are still very small, if they portend important consequences.[1]

An effective way to catch nasty long-term trends early is to use a highly disciplined and steady extrapolation procedure, one that becomes routine and is always ready, always focused, and always employed. Developing the habit of extrapolating early to disclose possibilities for later years can pay off.

INTRODUCING NEW PRODUCTS

Extrapolation can be valuable for improving earlier experiences with prediction. We demonstrate by considering a particular class of common prediction, namely, the scenario of progress when a company's new product is introduced. The forecast for a substantial period ahead for a new product might be as follows: The small initial sales, perhaps for a year or two, were anticipated as rising, but slowly, because the market would need time to become acquainted with the novel product. The rise in sales was then predicted to become steeper—indeed without such expectancy the new product would not have been chosen for production and marketing. The annual sales were then forecast to reach and maintain high annual rates, falling off in later years to a longer-term medium rate with a still later final period when sales would drop to a closeout ending.

The actual results would likely deviate somewhat from the originally predicted pattern. As the actuals are experienced, extrapolating should continue, with the forecast being regularly updated to be the most realistic for the future. The future projections should constitute the original plan modified and improved by continued extrapolating from the latest observed deviations from that plan. If the original forecast was far from being met, the extrapolated new possibilities for the period ahead would reflect that.

CYCLES EXTRAPOLATED: MODELS

Imagine a body of water good for commercial fishing where there were large fish and small fish. Fisherman A caught only the large fish while Fisherman B depended exclusively on the small fish. Fisherman A noted with satisfaction that his catch was growing steadily. At the same time Fisherman B had to make do with a daily decrease in what he brought in. Both were experienced, however, so neither one extrapolated the indefinite continuation of the two trends very far ahead. They knew the big fish were enthusiastically eating the small fish and hence thriving while the population of small fish, being eaten, was producing fewer offspring. Soon the big fish would be up against a food shortage, and the population of big fish, having reached a peak, would decline. The small fish, now diminished but not now being as likely to be eaten early, would commence a comeback, rising to a peak from which they too would decrease as the revived population of large fish again began to use the small ones as food.

The fishermen made their plans based on extrapolation from past to future. What they extrapolated, however, was not a straight line continuation but rather a long-term oscillating cycle. They used a model; they extrapolated a pattern of periodicity from the past to predict fish populations for decades ahead.

The foregoing story used a highly simplified model to make a point quickly. The real world of fishery would have required a much more complex long-term model because the two fish populations were not the only occupiers of the body of water and many other phenomena involved would affect the condition of the water and hence the fishing pattern over time. Model building is employed widely in numerous attempts at prediction. Basically, the use of computer-based prediction models is merely sophisticated extrapolation from past patterns of phenomena to future behavior.

This technique has been applied extensively in the field of economics, where very complex models have been designed. These models, unfortunately, have enjoyed only limited success. The important, interesting, and real-life economic phenomena are more complicated than it is usually practical to understand deeply enough to model. Economists seem to have developed considerable expertise in creating models that, had they been applied at the time, would have predicted past economic surprises (like the huge Depression starting in 1929). But today's best economic models do not usually work well enough to predict economic changes with justified confidence. Famous economist Alice Rivlin has been cited as doubting that we will ever see improved economics prediction because, she says, "it is too complicated."[2] When the Federal Reserve alters its interest rates, the rates on long-term bonds seem more often to surprise rather than adhere to predicted numbers. It is still often helpful, nevertheless, to employ models to uncover possibilities for economic trends. But the possibilities should be described by a wide band for each figure rather than by only one specific number (as will be further discussed in a later chapter).

QUALITATIVE EXTRAPOLATIONS

Extrapolation can be helpful in searching for possibilities worth listing not only as numbers quantitatively describing future activities but also as qualitative characteristics of what is ahead. For example, we have noted the tendency of leading companies to lose their positions by failing to see major changes coming in their own special fields. We described in Chapter 1 how Western Union missed telephony and how General Electric, the world's largest electric technology company for many decades, not only missed broadcast television's arrival but also failed to see semiconductors and computers as the next dominant pillars of its industry. Similarly, the giant retail merchandising chains that existed at the time did not foresee the innovative marketing approaches of a new competitor, Wal-Mart, which in a surprisingly short time passed them to become the world's largest retail chain. Today, some companies owning newspapers and other print media are handicapped by competition from ubiquitous online Internet delivery of information. (This does not apply to all such owners, because some also own new as well as older entities in information dissemination.)

A specific extrapolation procedure suggests itself from those past experiences: If you have been first in your field for decades, one long-term possibility you should list, by qualitative extrapolation, is that some competitor with a new approach—as to nature of product, manufacturing method, or marketing procedure—is likely to arise and take away your leadership position. If you have led your field for a long time, you should not assume as the sole possibility that you will do so forever. It is sensible to extrapolate past experience scenarios, not numbers alone, to picture possibilities for the future.

EXTRAPOLATING SURPRISES

Recent past history is sometimes a strong indication of a condition or of a trend that is likely to continue into the future. That is why extrapolation is at times very useful. But new occurrences that have just been experienced are often transients. The patterns, that is, will pass after only temporary and brief showings, so they will not be useful indicators for forecasting the long-term future. For example, consider the heated competition between Boeing and Airbus, the two principal suppliers of airplanes for large commercial airlines. In the three decades following America's victory in World War II, Boeing became the dominant world supplier. Then, for a while, Airbus became the triumphant competitor, winning the majority of annual sales. In the more immediate past, Boeing has again been the competition winner. Both results stemmed not from some long-term or cyclical phenomena but from short-lived, individual superior decisions or bad ones the two competitors took turns making about designing for the market, seemingly at random as to timing and not necessarily related to each other or inherent to either.

So we must always be careful not to extrapolate a change whenever we observe one, thinking we have spotted a continuing trend, when it actually may be only a short-term effect. Airbus may have made an error in staking too much on the expectancy that a huge airplane, one carrying some 600 to 700 people, would win quick acceptance by the airlines and it didn't. A few years earlier Boeing was seen by some critics as not well managed, and Airbus led in plane sales.

As they produce their forecasts, both Boeing and Airbus have needed to include the possibility of losing out to the other and will always attempt to understand why. The quality of the engineering, manufacturing, marketing skill, and the performance of the produced aircraft—these fundamentals will dominate the success of each company in the long run, and such basics are not always determined by extrapolating recent results.

If an area of activity has in the past been replete with bubbles and quickly passing phenomena, then the forecaster should consider—by extrapolation of past to future—that such transient effects will likely again appear. The forecaster should not be found amazed and unprepared when they surface. All predictors have the experience of coming up with some badly wrong long-term predictions. Expected events may fail to occur. Others that do happen may do so far earlier or much later than expected, or with repercussions much worse than forecast, or with benefits substantially superior to what was envisioned. Suppose the recent past of the activity for which you are engaged in providing forecasts has been dominated by a surprise. It could be an act of a cruel Mother Nature, like the recent dislocation of life by dry spells, floods, and winds. Or it could be the unexpected success of a competitor.

If the surprise is entirely beneficial to your operation, you will happily go about adjusting to the unexpected good news. If the surprise presents you with serious problems, however, you will likely find yourself with some questions, including extrapolation issues that should interest you greatly. Will the new, unanticipated situation continue? Will the surprising recent past characterize the period ahead?

Of course, you will endeavor to understand why you were surprised. That understanding, if you attain it, will influence your next long-term predictions. But one possibility you will surely want to consider is the simple extrapolation that the new, unexpected condition will continue. More complex extrapolation may be in order as you contemplate what will happen next. If what has occurred is very different from your anticipations, what other surprises might await you? The events that previously escaped your forecasting may suggest specific other events to follow that you also are not yet including in your predicting. If the world economy in late 2008 was a surprise, what might you now expect in the years to follow? Were you shocked by what a competitor accomplished? Then you should not be shocked by a competitor's further success in the future. What might that competitor, or a different one, do next? Whatever the surprise was, if bad, will it get worse? If bringing democracy to a country that has never known it causes the population to elect terrorists to power—a surprise to the United States in the Gaza Strip—should not the same result be a possibility if the United States attempts to establish a democracy somewhere else?

Sometimes a period of inaccuracy of prediction performance should be extrapolated; that is, the same level of inaccuracy should be considered as a possibility for the future. In particular, specific kinds of deviations from perfect prediction may well be integral to the predictor. It is reasonable to include the possibility that the particular characteristics of a predictor that showed up in past bad predictions may characterize, at least somewhat, that predictor's future predictions. Thus, if you have shown yourself very often to be overly optimistic, you should consider extrapolating this as inherent to your personality. So when your prediction is about to be completed, you perhaps should inject some pessimism as a final touch. After adding this correction step, you will note the results. Do your forecasts now turn out to be more accurate?

Analyze your record of prediction imperfections and extrapolate a continuation of your indulging in them if you do nothing. Contemplating that poor future forecasting may lead to your improving your predicting.

INNOVATIVE EXTRAPOLATING

Numerous ways exist of employing more complex extrapolations as a means of disclosing possibilities. An imaginative extrapolation can be stimulating and useful in an interesting way. It may have as its main purpose to force thinking about possibilities you would miss unless you were willing to use your imagination, even chancing not being totally on solid ground. Our friend James Hodgson's experience doing college homework before World War II will illustrate this.[3] A student in the 1930s, he was assigned to do a term paper on disarmament. So he went to the library, and, using the *Periodicals Index*, he compiled a list of published articles with "disarmament" in the title, starting with 1919 when World War I ended. The list grew longer each year, peaked in 1924 (the year of the historic International Disarmament Conference), and then began down, he observed. He also noted that as time passed, the word "peace" began to appear in titles coupled with "disarmament." So he decided to also plot the number of articles annually that included the word "peace." This number also grew and peaked (in 1928, the year of the Kellogg-Briand Pact). Then he saw that "war" began to appear in titles along with "peace," so he plotted "war." Again, as this quantity appeared, it began heading upward.

We can readily understand when Hodgson then "made a quantum leap into the unknown," as he described it. He could not resist hypothesizing thusly: Both "disarmament" and "peace" citings had risen and peaked, the latter reaching a higher level than the former but on a curve similarly shaped. "War," he thought, might also peak on a similarly shaped curve and at a still higher level. What would the date of that peaking represent? An outbreak of war perhaps? Curious and mischievously daring, Hodgson placed two additions on his graph. One was a line through the two peaking points of "disarmament" and "peace" with the possibility that the expected "war" peak, when it occurred, might fall on that rising line. The other was an extension and completion of the "war" citings curve so that its shape would match in form the rise and fall of the "disarmament" and "peace" curves. The extrapolated "peaking points" line and the extrapolated "war" curve intersected. Did the date of that intersection constitute a prediction? Of what? Of the next war perhaps? The intersection happened to fall in the second half of 1939. Hitler invaded Poland in September of that year.

This example is not offered, of course, as evidence that World War II's opening date in 1939 was predicted correctly by this student's extrapolation in 1936. But citing this bit of bold extrapolating suggests it is sometimes interesting to experiment with extrapolating innovatively with little inhibition, thus hoping to suggest possibilities that otherwise might not come to mind. Outlandishly conjured up possibilities obviously would deserve to be dismissed immediately when they clearly possess little foundation or violate common sense or lead to easily seen impossibilities. But sometimes even wildly extrapolated possibilities might be difficult to reject quickly and entirely, because something about them hints that they may have a serious, real component.

EXTRAPOLATION AS A MANAGEMENT TOOL

Let us return for a moment to the case of the extreme loss of product market share described early in this chapter. If you are the manager, you will surely ask why so great a loss has happened, and the conceivable reasons might well be seen as numerous. Has your selling price been carelessly set higher than the competitor's price, and the competitor has found that, with its lower price, it could take market share away from you and still be adequately profitable? Has the competitor improved its product over yours? Has your research and development budget been too low? Has the competitor been more innovative in marketing or in manufacturing? Are its costs lower? If so, why? Pertinent questions about the actions of competitors always merit analysis; they will often arise more quickly as a result of extrapolating.

An array of factors characterizes the operations of all managed entities, be they businesses, government departments, colleges, hospitals, or charities. Companies typically record revenues, costs, inventories, net earnings, and more for all profit centers. But it is not common to compute and record rates of changes regarding all the main figures that categorize the activity and extrapolate them so as to picture possibilities. "Business today is awash in data and data crunchers, but only certain companies have transformed this technology from a supporting tool into a strategic weapon. Their ability to collect, analyze and act on data is the essence of their competitive advantage and the source of their superior performance."[4]

How far to go in amassing and analyzing data from earlier periods depends ultimately, of course, on management's perceived value of having the results available as management tools. But extrapolation in particular, if it is to aid in compiling a useful list of future possibilities, will be impaired if the data on the past and present and the study of the implications of the data are both too skimpy.

Practicing extrapolation not only can provide management with a broader compendium of possibilities worthy of consideration but can also help managers to do something intelligent about those possibilities. If the return on investment in a particular area of your business appears headed downward, you will want to know why and what you can do about it. If student applications to the college you are managing are rising, should you consider raising tuition? If you are losing employees to a competitor, should you consider increasing salaries? If things did not go as forecast, the data should help you figure out why. Of course, as you plan your future operations, you should not depend on the use of formal extrapolation techniques as the only aid. Fortunately, the data collection needed for useful extrapolation will be helpful for all aspects of management.

Chapter Five | Possibility Generators

We emphasize again that for success in creating useful predictions, the best beginning is to list future possibilities. Extrapolating, we have noted, is an important way to generate them. There are many other generators of valuable possibilities. In this chapter we discuss a number of them.

MISSING LINKS

Some imaginable future developments that could have important consequences are not listed because missing links seem clearly to preclude such developments from coming to pass. Often, however, the missing links can be identified clearly and speculation about them can lead to possibilities worth listing. Example: There is enough coal underground in the United States to eliminate the problem of shortages of crude oil and its resulting high price—this if only we have a cheap, reliable, and environmentally clean way to turn solid hard coal into a liquid to fuel our autos and trucks.[1] Such means is a missing link today. We must ask if a possibility exists that this identified link might show up.

We risk being overly imaginative to make a point here. Imagine we set off an atom bomb in the center of a very large and deep coal deposit, which explosion creates a spherical hole there. The enormous pressure from the explosion causes the hole to fill with liquid that has been squeezed out of the surrounding coal. This liquid fuel is then pumped out and, behold, the missing link has arrived![2] This approach might apply as well to forcing liquid petroleum out of the rich shale deposits in Colorado and Canada. Perhaps?

The coming of the computer age, with its multi-billion-dollar impact on the world economy, could have been regarded long ago as certain to emerge if and when an answer were to surface to what was then a clear missing link. This was a replacement for the vacuum tube at once very much smaller and more reliable, with longer life, generating trivial heat, and lending itself to low-price mass production. That missing link, the semiconductor, did indeed emerge, and it was followed by the information technology revolution that has affected all aspects of life on Earth.

Many examples of today's missing links abound. As noted in an earlier chapter, there is frequent mention of hydrogen as a future energy source. Hydrogen-operated autos could reduce to minor the United States' need for foreign oil and the environmental damage arising from operating cars and trucks. (The exhaust gas would be water vapor.) This would be a tremendous development. But needed are the presently not available safe, lightweight, and economically feasible means to extract, store, and transport hydrogen. Hydrogen can be derived from petroleum, but that obviously must be ruled out. It also can be obtained from water, but doing so requires too much electric power. Could hydrogen be separated from water by use of sunlight? Some prominent scientists think so.[3] That would provide the missing link. (See also Chapter 13 of this book.)

Means vastly superior to present batteries for storage of electricity with much more capacity at less weight and size, at a lower price, and with a greater life if suddenly no longer missing would impact radically the design of vehicles. Interest in electric cars has already risen greatly in the past few years when superior batteries became available, but a fundamental breakthrough beyond the battery approach for electric energy storage has still not arrived, although some possibilities have surfaced.[4]

The Sun deposits over 100,000 times more energy on Earth than the population employs. Thus it is more than a little tempting to seek ways to solve all our energy requirements by making more use of sunlight. Solar generators, using the Sun's rays to generate electricity, tantalizingly borders on being a practical answer to the desire for a nonfuel and noncombustion energy source. But no operation at night and on cloudy days means that an acceptable solar energy system is handicapped for too many applications by lack of good electricity storage means. That is one of the missing links in achieving a solar energy solution. (Chapter 13 of this book deals further with this.)

Missing solutions to technical problems hold back controlled nuclear fusion (the physical process basic to the hydrogen bomb) that in principle could lead to plentiful and cheap energy. Wind power is a means of generating electricity handicapped by a missing link, how to store the energy created when the wind blows so that it can be available while the blowing stops as it is inclined to do part of the time. (That link is not missing in Norway where there are many hydroelectric plants and where wind power, when available, is used to pump water up to reservoir levels. The system uses the high-level water to drive turbine generators that supply electric power needs during windless periods.)

The missing link concept is not limited to technology breakthroughs. The long-term price of crude oil makes it sensible to consider biofuels as a substitute for petroleum. Ethanol can be derived from corn and other plant matter, and biodiesel from soybeans. Cellulosic ethanol, perhaps its most attractive variety, can be produced from certain grasses rich in cellulose. These nonfossil sources are proven substitutes for gasoline and ordinary diesel fuels. However, with oil at $20 or even $50 a barrel, the price of shifting to biofuels is not economically sound. That is, the investment to reach an adequate supply of biofuel for the United States by an enormous expansion of growing and processing facilities in this country or arranging to obtain it from other countries is too high. At $100 a barrel for oil, however, it is a different matter. The missing link, so that biofuel can help reduce our dependence on foreign crude oil, may be a steady oil price of $100 per barrel.

Ethanol made from food crops like maize yields only 30 percent more energy than that required to produce the ethanol. But ethanol made from trees can produce over 30 times as much energy as is required to create it. The trouble is trees take much more time to grow than grass or food crops. The missing link is fast-growing trees.

Most biofuels, even those thought serious candidates as substitutes for petroleum imports, are replete with missing links.

The oil substitutes that presently come from corn, soy, sugar cane, or trees are relatively expensive, need intensive agriculture effort, threaten food supplies, and use too much energy, land, and water for the many operating steps. A missing link is an agricultural product far superior in the critical fundamentals. Recently, an Australian professor has proposed the jatropha plant.[5] It favors the hot and dry conditions that many underdeveloped tropical countries possess (along with plentiful poverty, hence low-cost labor). Jatropha is not edible; therefore, its use for fuel does not diminish food supply. It contains an oil that can be turned into biodiesel by economic means. This is already being done in India far more efficiently than using corn, and it requires less water as well. Jatropha is perhaps an answer to the missing link in the bio-fuel category.

In summary, predictors of long-term, broad developments in society must steadily ask themselves: What critical needed elements appear unavailable today that, if they were to suddenly appear, would make an enormous difference? Why have they not yet surfaced? What holds them up? What would have to change so those missing links would emerge? What might then happen? What can we do to accelerate the process? And, finally, are possibilities on this front worth listing as we try to predict and shape the future?

SURE THINGS

As we have already noted, the possibility should always be taken seriously that your predictions may be badly off. Are you perhaps very certain a particular possibility is likely? Then be sure to ask yourself why you are so sure. Identify the reasons and try taking each reason apart relentlessly. What would have to change to cause your safe prediction to be in error? A competitor with a radically new idea might create havoc. A war might alter your basic assumptions. Continued collapse of the world economy seems to some to be a sure thing. Yet, perhaps competent government action might prevent it. In listing possibilities, challenge your most confident assumptions before you consider your list of possibilities to be complete. Doing this may generate more possibilities.

SCIENCE AND TECHNOLOGY ADVANCES

No reader of this book needs to be told that the world will be altered by future science and technology advances, not all of which can be anticipated. The technical publications are full of descriptions of possibilities as is the business press and the mass media. The promises and expectancies are important not only to highly technological industries. In one way or another, directly or indirectly, these advances impact every activity from manufacturing to transportation, health care, education, security, and entertainment. The spectrum of science and technology advances is so broad that it may seem hopeless to pick out possibilities that are realistic, sensible choices for your particular field of endeavor. But not everything important in your field should be assumed too difficult to analyze.

Consider how potential advances in agricultural technology in the United States could have been listed as a possibility during the early decades of the twentieth century by only superficially knowledgeable experts. They could have seen that technology advances would come to have a tremendous impact on the growing of food. Simultaneous progress in farm machinery, soil fertilization, insecticides, dam design, irrigation methods, flood control, and plant science could have been expected to make possible great future increases in yield, a positive balance of trade, a shrinking need for workers on farms, a developing farm surplus problem, and farm hands moving to seek jobs in the cities. Such early predicting, had it been accomplished a hundred years ago, probably would have been off in timing details and in various other important aspects. Even had predictions made then been perfect, they probably would not have been taken seriously by the society; it was far from accustomed then to taking advantage of such anticipating. But good predictors could have "separated the wheat from the chaff" and beneficially influenced their future.

It is not difficult today to describe many science fields in which the probabilities of great advances affecting humankind appear high. In some instances these perceived likelihoods stem from credible scientific theories and discoveries not yet fully exploited as aids to invention. In others, new observations and measurements of natural phenomena over broader ranges of conditions suggest rapid future science and technology progress.

Thus, theories today about the forming of the Earth's continents and the causes of earthquakes, together with heightened ability to record movements of the Earth's crust, suggest that reliable, usefully accurate earthquake prediction might well come about in the future. It is also to be expected that social adjustment to improved earthquake prediction will turn out to be difficult. For example, how should we handle a possible mass exodus from a region in response to an earthquake alarm that might be either a false alarm or the real thing?

Certain aspects of weather forecasting—and even weather modification—should be listed as ready for a mass build-up of its scientific foundations. For the first time, as mentioned earlier, simultaneous observations can be made from space, in the atmosphere, and on land and the oceans. These observations can be brought together in real time, and improved understanding of the interactions of the various phenomena can be reached. With the cupboard in which these weather secrets are locked now about to open, it should be assumed that the shelves will not be found bare but rather full of significant discoveries. A consequent possibility might be to become capable of acting ahead to limit floods, hurricanes, and other weather disasters by the use of properly designed and placed weather-altering nuclear energy injections in the skies.

The field of microbiology has moved today into a favored position with anticipation of great advances much in evidence. The fundamentals of living matter are being probed and comprehended at the molecular level. The human gene has been mapped and sequenced. Manipulating genes may lead to the power to reorganize the matter forming all living organisms. Stem cells may be developable into needed human body parts. Press leading microbiologists only slightly and they will describe possible "imminent breakthroughs" with tremendous potential for prevention and curing of diseases. This will affect everything on Earth.

GOVERNMENT ACTIONS

Any manager engaged in listing future possibilities as a step toward attaining useful predictions must include potential government actions. American voters are well aware that substantive effort must be attempted by the Congress and the president if severe and growing problems are to be diminished. Examples of these well-identified problems are in areas of immigration, health care, treatment for drug addiction, protection of the environment, K-12 education, reduction of dependence on foreign oil, improvement of the nation's economy, and prevention of homeland terrorism.

One possibility is that the government will accomplish little of significance in the foreseeable future about such enormously difficult problems because they are so heavily loaded with dilemmas and insoluble facets.[6] But U.S. voters are becoming aware of the likely unacceptably bad effects of these festering problems on their nation's future economic strength and security and on their children because of the government's failure to act. For the United States to merit often the lowest rating among the world's developed nations in the education of its children is increasingly viewed as catastrophic by the country's voters. Something similar can be said of our inadequate health care services. Accordingly, it is possible that in the coming years, politicians will find their chances for election to be based not only on their promises to attack these problems but on their records of effective progress.

Of course, for every government attempt at problem solutions, the possibility exists of a failure of the approach. We must recall the famous economist Milton Friedman's oft-cited rule that whenever the government tries to solve a problem of the nation, it makes it worse. (We assume a "poetic license" of deliberate exaggeration by Friedman.) Prohibition as a cure for alcoholism was later seen as more penalizing to the nation than the disease, so prohibition was abolished. A massive national welfare system may have institutionalized, not ameliorated, our nation's economic underclass. Many believe the U.S. government's recent involvement with K-12 education has hurt it, not helped it. The federal government has subsidized efforts to produce ethanol from corn, this to decrease the need for huge petroleum imports. But one effect has been to drive up corn prices, creating handicaps for pork producers, chicken farmers, and dairies. (Livestock owners cannot feed their animals at doubled corn prices.) The huge requirements for land and water if the government persists in sponsoring ethanol production may force it to abandon the program.

The Sarbanes-Oxley Act (SOX) was created because of crimes by a small number of corporation executives. It is now seen, however, that enormous new expenses have been created by SOX for corporations, accounting companies, law firms, and banks as they have sought to meet the stringent data gathering and reporting requirements of the act. Some have suggested that these costs might well now exceed the amount of future scandal damages the act was created to halt.[7] Others believe SOX might be driving new investments from the public market to the private equity market.

Company executives and auditors are hard-pressed to fully understand all of the accounting pronouncements now coming out of the Federal Accounting Standards Board (FASB) at a remarkable rate. Many of them are over 50 pages in length with accompanying interpretations 10 times longer. Auditors are increasingly unwilling to offer interpretations of such new rules; they are rather more likely to apply rules in the most severe way possible out of fear of shareholder lawsuits or jail sentences. Consequently, many publicly traded companies have been issuing restatements of previously reported results. There may not be enough accountants to staff these broadened audits. Costs have been driven up greatly. Most troubling, the deluge of new accounting rules may well serve to make financial statements and proxy disclosures more confusing than before. A major streamlining of SOX appears to be needed.

If you are seeking to predict future government endeavors, you must seek answers to such questions as these: What new requirements might the government implement in the coming years? What might be the results, good or bad? How will that alter, both as to problems and opportunities, the situation in the area of the society you are managing? You must ponder ahead of time what the government might do, particularly about the economy, because you cannot be satisfied merely to react after that action has been taken.

MERGING AND ACQUIRING

The operating patterns of business organizations are constantly changing. Some developments happen in response to new actions by governments. Other deviations from past practices are made by industry to exploit fresh markets and science and technology advances. Still others are adjustments to solve problems and take advantage of opportunities stemming from business expansion internationally. Wars, stock market crashes, and environmental and health disasters can alter the conditions under which businesses function. When the leaders of businesses attempt the intelligent identifying of coming possibilities for their businesses' futures, they must list possible changes in the basic business environment.

We illustrate this first with the example of the growing boom in mergers and acquisitions (M&As) by business organizations. M&A activity, now increasingly international, has reached the level of hundreds of billions of dollars per year. When as a company executive you attempt to foresee the period ahead, you will give ample weight, of course, to mergers and acquisitions activities already in process. You must also force yourself to speculate about M&A possibilities that have not yet surfaced or perhaps have not yet even been conceived. Too often companies that become acquiree candidates are taken by surprise. If that should happen to the business corporation of which you are a principal executive, then in a frenzy you might find yourself defending against a takeover. Or, in contrast, you might have to act quickly to outbid a competitor who suddenly is intent on buying some third company that you now see you should have considered acquiring.

Belatedly you may realize you should have envisaged more M&A possibilities earlier. Such possibilities should be rated as to probability, timing, and benefits to shareholders and employees. You should be imaginative as you ask yourself what M&A activity deserves effort to shape the future.

You should give special attention to competitors. Might they initiate M&A activities that could affect your operation? Might it be advantageous to you to consider such possibilities even though it is competitors who might take the initiative and not you? Specifically, you should even include the possibility that it may be best for your shareholders that you sell out to others.

PRIVATIZING

Another business change phenomenon that you should mull over as a deserving source of possibilities for your business's future is "going private." Publicly held corporations have become attractive for purchase by private equity funds. These risk takers expect to be able to make a company's value grow greatly and reap the consequent rewards. Their reasons include the following:

- They will not need to issue public quarterly financial reports that must meet external analysts' expectations; they can rather make long-term restructuring and investment decisions.
- They can operate with a higher debt-to-equity ratio than is considered sound for publicly held corporations.
- They can change management, make mergers and acquisitions, drop unproductive activities, and generally alter a company's goals and priorities without the handicap of needing to seek shareholders' approvals.
- They will be less encumbered by costly, burdensome reporting requirements that delay and limit the actions of public, but not private, corporations (such as those mandated, for example, by the Sarbanes-Oxley Act).

Over the last few decades, private equity funds have enjoyed annual rates of return well exceeding the average of publicly held corporations. If you are listing future possibilities for your business, you must include your company's being taken private, or your company's arranging to go private, or one of your competitors' becoming private.

Of course, when you identify the possibility that your company might become a private entity, it does not necessarily have to apply to the whole company. Consider, for example, the following possibility: Your corporation is developing an exciting new product; but you are forced to do so slowly, on a tight budget. This is because in going faster, the expense will hurt your earnings substantially in the near term and you know that will be highly unsatisfactory to your shareholders. A private venture fund offers to buy that new product activity from you—your company still retaining a significant fraction—and plans then to finance a new private corporation to develop the new product and market it. This will be at a high speed to prevent competitors from arising and beating the new entity to market. You decide the arrangement is best for your shareholders. So now you put this possibility on your list with a high probability that if implemented it will lead to a successfully realized prediction. (A bad possibility that you might be wise to turn into a prediction if you don't act is that your key people developing this new product area might leave you to create a new company financed by outside venture funds to bring the new product to market well ahead of you.)

SELF-FULFILLING NEGATIVE PROPHECIES

If you began smoking as a child, have been a chain-smoker since, and plan never to quit, you might predict that you will not live as long as your former schoolmates who have never smoked. Chances are that your prediction will come true. It is a self-fulfilling prophecy.

Sometimes you see an interesting possible future development that you know will not happen unless another development occurs first. Both possibilities appear, however, to have little chance of actually coming about. This contingency-based happening, whose probability involves multiplying two numbers, each much smaller than 1.0, results in a greatly reduced overall probability. (If each possibility has 1 chance in 10 of occurring, then the chances of both happening are 1 in 100.) Example: The development of the often described hydrogen-fueled automobile depends on the development of practical, safe, and economic means for producing, transporting, and storing hydrogen.

An excellent report card on the accuracy of predictions can result from employing a totally negative approach to problems even when their seriousness is well identified. If you see bad developments ahead and do nothing to prevent their occurring, then you should predict they will. As a predictor, your score will be excellent. To operate this way, however, is not the common approach of a competent manager although it is hardly a rare modus operandi when it comes to the leading of nations. For example, it is now accepted that strength in science and technology is required to ensure security, economic stability, and improvement in average living standards. Accordingly, any nation that lowers its priority and support for education and for science and technology advances can predict a lowering of its future status among the advanced nations of the world. That prediction will turn out to be accurate, an instance of a negative self-fulfilled prophecy.

After the World War II, the United States clearly became the leading technological nation. We led in research and development (R&D), and our highly innovative manufacturing methods created productivity advances that enabled us to outcompete nations with lower labor costs. For decades we were first in almost all science and engineering fields. But now the U.S. government's investment in physical science research as a fraction of gross domestic product (GDP) is down to half of what it was four decades ago. In China, R&D rose 350 percent in the same period, and the number of Ph.D.s in science and engineering China produced increased by 500 percent. Not surprisingly, the number of patents filed in the United States by Chinese scientists and engineers has increased by 400 percent. Our top graduate schools used to attract the pick of students from nations all over the globe, many of whom later became American citizens. After 9/11, delays in processing student visas have caused the number of graduate students from elsewhere to be down to a third of the earlier years' figures.[8]

We are no longer acting to ensure the strength of our science and technology leadership.[9] If we do not change what has become the U.S. practice, we can accurately predict that while this nation's capabilities will remain strong, the United States will no longer be the world leader.

The United States has a number of critical problems that will surely get worse unless concerted, effective national government action is undertaken to lessen them. Illegal immigration, lack of protection of the environment, continued dependence on imports of petroleum, and inadequate medical care, as well as poor education and less scientific research, can easily be predicted to lessen the quality of life of the average U.S. citizen. The government, it appears now, will continue to be handicapped in solving these problems by political partisanship, bureaucracy, selfish interests, and especially, a lack of practical ideas and adequate leadership. Negative consequences seem extremely likely.

But what of the contributions of the private sector? Unfortunately, the technological industry is also a plentiful producer of negative possibilities. In recent years, Wall Street and the business media have put overwhelming emphasis on quarterly reports when rating corporate performance. That equates to demanding short-term, steady earnings growth that is at odds with long-term investment in technology advance, which, to create major new products, typically requires decades, not years. Not only the CEOs but also the decision makers at executive levels well below are likely to be loath to schedule R&D expenses that will hurt the near term's earnings and the stock prices. After all, the possible but much later benefits will seem to advance only the statures, salaries, and bonuses of their successors rather than themselves. This is especially true for those in corporate management when their ages reach the upper fifties or the sixties, particularly if the retirement age is 65.

Einstein is quoted as having written, "Life is like riding a bicycle. To keep your balance you must keep moving."[10] If you are the decision maker in a business of any kind and you do not keep moving—that is, you take no risks and institute no changes—then there is a good possibility you will be guaranteeing a self-fulfilled prophecy of your company's future failure to hold its position against competitors as the world, in contrast, moves forward.

SUDDEN DISCONTINUITIES

Unfortunately for the performance record of would-be successful predictors of long-range future developments, many important occurrences surface with little warning. They arrive as sudden discontinuities, unexpected departures from what has been happening, and they cause the future to be startlingly different from the past—like the 2008 world economy disaster. That does not mean they should all be regarded as having been "unpredictable." When studied later, they sometimes appear better labeled simply "unpredicted."

Consider, for example, the Japanese attack on Pearl Harbor and the war that followed and ended with atom bombs dropped on the Japanese homeland. Was this not a perfect example of sudden, unpredictable discontinuities in world events? No. Before deciding to attack Pearl Harbor, the Japanese leadership, we should presume, performed what they regarded as a profound study of the possible consequences of that attack. As a prediction start, Japan's leaders may have surmised that they might be seen by the world as justified in conceiving East Asia—China and adjacent areas—as territory that deserved to be dominated by them, much as such a position had been more or less long accepted for the United States regarding the American continents. But with the United States' clearly appearing unwilling to allow the Japanese this "natural" role, the Japanese accordingly felt they must somehow cause the United States to do so, employing force if necessary. Certainly, moreover, the various actions by the United States to handicap Japan in its acquiring such strategic commodities as oil must have caused Japan to accept the risk, as absolutely necessary, of its attempting to neutralize the American fleet in Hawaii.

To the Japanese in 1940 and 1941 it might have seemed a safe prediction that America would rate the saving of Britain and the defeat of Hitler as meriting much higher priority than interfering with Japan's plans in Asia. And with Hitler assumed at that time virtually certain to be in control of Europe from the Atlantic to the Urals, he could be beaten—Japan's leaders might well have predicted—only through landing a massive U.S. army in Europe. In such an attempt Hitler would possess comparable, if not greater, military resources and could exploit the tremendous advantage of defense over offense against an invader trying large-scale landings against a highly fortified coast in almost permanently bad coastal weather. After many disastrous attempts to establish a major force in Europe, with casualties in the millions, the United States was likely predicted by Japan as forced to give up on ousting Hitler.

Furthermore, it might well have been prophesized by Japan that the U.S. leadership would be unable to justify to its citizens the terrible price of trying to contest Japan's control of Asia. In fact, at that time Japan's military was larger, better trained, and better equipped than America's. The United States, Japan likely believed, would realize quickly that for ultimate success its forces eventually would have to occupy Japan's far-away home country. Japan naturally felt certain it could seize and fortify heavily the Philippines and all other islands in the Pacific that might offer the United States necessary staging areas for the huge armies required to attempt invading Japan. The United States, if it tried to land forces in Japan, would undergo unacceptable mass casualties—and all that with no certainty of success—in fact, highly probably, with disastrous failure.

Accordingly, Japan's predictors must have concluded confidently that Japan should attack Pearl Harbor. They could thereby destroy much of the U.S. Navy, making clear to the Americans from the outset that a U.S.-Japanese war could only become an unacceptable stalemate for the United States. An eventual peace deal, one highly unfavorable to the United States, probably was forecast by Japan as the certain way that war would end, with the United States' having to recognize East Asia as coming under Japanese supervision for the foreseeable future.

But this prediction by Japan, if it actually was made, turned out to be fatally wrong because Japan failed to list four possibilities: (1) Hitler's plans for capturing the USSR's resources might fail. (2) The will of the American people to fight was huge. (3) The industrial capacity of an awakened America was enormous. (4) The United States developed and utilized the atom bomb, and this powerful technology's becoming available to the United States constituted a discontinuity of overwhelming influence.

The U.S. leadership should have expected the Pearl Harbor attack. The above described prediction rationale of Japan's government in planning and executing that attack should have been listed as a strong possibility by American predictors. They had only to imagine themselves in the position of Japan's leaders and to take into consideration the existence of Japan's large fleet of aircraft carriers, which was well known to the United States.

Could not Japan's nuclear physicists (they had some) have listed in 1940 and 1941 the United States' coming development of an atom bomb as a serious possibility? In the 1930s and early

1940s, there had been much open discussion in the world's physics fraternity of the potential releasing of energy from nuclear reactions. Most top nuclear researchers believed an atom bomb of unprecedented power could indeed be developed. Japanese scientists could have informed the Japanese leadership of this possibility. The American scientists were so confident of success that they pushed hard for the Manhattan project's initiation because of fear the Germans might attain that awesome capability first.

PREDICTABLE SURPRISES

The arrival of atom bombs was rated sudden and unexpected by most.[11] So was the later collapse of the USSR. So also was the amazing penetration of the World Trade Center buildings by captured, fully fueled airliners piloted by suicidal terrorists. But not all unforeseen events important to would-be long-range predictors have been sudden in their arrival. Some have been years in forming and have dropped important clues during that period. When they came about, they should not have been considered shocking. The failure to have seen those events as possibilities and so not acting early was extremely regrettable. For example, foreign manufacturers' taking over so much of the American automotive market was not a sharp, abrupt event. It took decades, during most of which time the American producers seemingly never expected their losses of market share to go so far. Should not the breakdown of the home mortgage business in 2008 been seen as a strong possibility years before it occurred?

Predictors must seek to move the big future discontinuities from the classification of unpredictables to that of possibilities.

MAKING IT HAPPEN

The most satisfying prediction adventure a leader can experience is to visualize a great, exciting future possibility, see a way to make it happen, and, finally, cause it to occur, truly shaping the future. It need not be a phenomenal new product based on a spectacular technology advance or scientific discovery. It can be a novel way of marketing or manufacturing or handling information or providing a service, one needed by society but one that others have not previously perceived, realizing neither that the need exists nor how to fill it.

The visualization of something of important value and of a way to provide it is not limited to the creating or running of a business. We illustrate this with an example far removed from the industry side of life. A half century ago, some Los Angeles leaders predicted that the city's population had grown multidimensionally enough so that if they created a "music center"—replete with a top symphony orchestra, a grand opera company, and a playhouse devoted to new plays and musicals—people would come. Despite the many who, upon hearing of the proposal, said it would not work and should not be attempted, those leaders predicted the funds could be raised to build it; they went on to organize the effort, and they made it happen. The people who donated the funds and the city and county officials who had to approve the plan and make the land available believed the prediction that the result would be a successful step for the city. The predictors had presented a detailed plan that rang with credibility. The predictors made the Los Angeles Music Center happen. It was a self-fulfilled prophecy. They shaped the future.

Over a century ago Henry Ford saw the possibility of designing, producing, and selling an automobile that would be simple enough and low enough in price to fill a societal need and wish. He combined the prediction that it could be done with remarkable innovations in design of the vehicle and the way it was manufactured. He moved from the possibility to the details of actually transforming it from a vision to a reality.

In recent decades the leading entrepreneurs in semiconductors and computers looked ahead and visualized possibilities that (perhaps strangely, perhaps as could be expected) the existing entrenched large companies failed to perceive. The founders of the new start-ups accompanied their predictions with the right actions to make the predictions happen.

Whether you lead a manufacturer, a clinic, an Internet service, a school system, or a theater chain, you must never think your list of future possibilities is complete unless you have included at least one very attractive possibility that you can turn into an actuality. This is an effort in which the functions of conjuring up possibilities, planning, forecasting, and accomplishing are all bound together.

Chapter Six | Predicting Big Externalities

Let us suppose you are a leader in your business and therefore are anxious also to be a competent predictor. You know well the issues influential in determining the future of your field. You also understand that the quality of your forecasting and the future of your entity will be determined not only by your level of understanding of the details of your area of operation but also by the goings-on in the outside world. But these external activities are unfortunately beyond the scope of your expertise and of your power to alter them. We shall refer to these important issues as *Big Externalities*.

Thus, if you are in the housing construction business, you will know that interest rates have a great deal to do with action in the home mortgages field and hence that they will affect your business. But you will also realize that your personal efforts can have only a negligible effect on the inflation rate of the economy or on the interest rates set by the Federal Reserve Board, two major influences on mortgage rates. Such Big Externalities will impinge on the accuracy of your predictions about future sales and earnings, but the particulars of those outside issues are not usually part of the information flow coming your way. Even if that input were complete, you possess limited ability to draw conclusions from the data so as to benefit your forecasting. Yet to shape the future, you must forecast it. How can you do that forecasting intelligently?

THE COMPLEXITY FACTOR

At the outset it is necessary to accept that the external phenomena bearing upon your activity and demanding consideration will not consist of a single issue, but rather of many. And, as to how these issues tie in to your activity, most often that connection will be broad, indirect, and subtle. The list will include the growth of the GNP of the United States, its unemployment rate, the cost of fighting terrorism, which political party will next control Congress, and how high the stock market might reach. To make matters more perplexing, these many separate contributing factors are not always measurable, and sometimes they are not even clearly defined. It is thus exceedingly difficult to pin down the potencies of their influences so as to gauge the extent to which they will participate in determining the future you are anxious to shape.[1]

Finally, those externalities generally interact with each other, one affecting the characteristics and status of another with their interrelationships usually far from clear. For example, the U.S. federal government's defense expenditures, the price of a barrel of oil, the foreign policies of the Western European nations, and the status of the warfare in Iraq are very different one from another, but they all participate in setting the total U.S. budget deficit. They relate to and influence each other, but never in a straightforward way that leads reliably to better predictions.

The just described complexity of external phenomena, when we try to include them in our forecasting, naturally can lead to wrong forecasts. The best experts' brains will not be capable of processing all the incompletely evaluated and indefinitely connected pieces of the total ensemble of externality issues. No expert will be skilled enough to produce a record of consistently accurate predictions. As a predictor, you must expect that. As a final disturbing fact, while we would hope to rely on experts for the understanding of such issues, they most often annoyingly differ widely. On almost any factor worth pondering in an endeavor to predict the effects of externalities accurately—America's productivity gain in the year ahead, or the possibility of a war's breaking out somewhere, or the likelihood of still another airline's filing for bankruptcy, or the growth of trade with India in the next decade—experts will disagree. If they have used elaborate computer models to broaden their inclusion and consideration of pertinent issues, they are likely to differ even more.

Nassim Nicholas Taleb claims that the gain over time in our ability to model and predict the world may be dwarfed by the rise in its complexity, this implying increasing influence of the unpredicted.[2]

PREDICTION RANGES

To obtain something valuable from prediction exercises despite this complexity is a challenge. Fortunately, for useful forecasting it is not always necessary to end with a single solid number or a yes or no answer—like the trade with Mexico will be a specific number of dollars next year, or a war in a certain world region will commence within two years, or a particular political party will control the Senate after the next election. We can produce valuable forecasts by estimating and employing a range, or spread, of possible future results. When predicting Big Externalities, a range is the prediction answer to be sought. For instance, we might forecast that unemployment in a particular industry or geographical area will be between 4 and 5 percent. Or that the probability of a certain event's occurring will lie between 50-50 and 60-40. The experts differ, let us say, as to the U.S. inflation rate for next year, some experts expecting it to be 1 percent while others predicting it to be 2 percent. However, we may feel quite confident that the inflation rate will not turn out to be below 1 percent—say, 0.5 percent—or above 2 percent—say, 3 percent. The experts' announcements, in other words, would justify our predicting that the ratio is likely to turn out to be between 1 and 2 percent.

Having predicted the range, we then can examine the possible consequences to the future of our own particular activity at each limit with confidence that we probably have covered the situation, certainly not completely, or maybe not even adequately, but at least somewhat usefully. If either of the two limits were to occur and if we had earlier concluded that we could not survive with one, or worse, with either, then the forecasting process already will have been of some help to us in our management duties because we might have acted earlier to better the future as a result of our prediction attempts.

We can look at it another way. Suppose we were to insist on choosing for prediction purposes a single number instead of a range, or a single answer to a Big Externalities issue (like there will be no war), while at the same time we know we lack the ability to arrive at so precise an answer. Then we would have kidded ourselves. We would be likely to end with a misleading forecast, the opposite of what we sought when engaging in a forecasting effort in the first place.

So, for predicting Big Externalities, think ranges.[3] How then to choose a range for an externality item needed for intelligent forecasting? To start with, the prediction team requires certain minimum efforts and abilities. If the entity for which the forecasting is being attempted is small, one person alone may constitute the entire prediction team. If the entity is large, it is more likely that several individuals with varied interests and experiences will be involved cooperatively in attempts to list those external issues most likely to affect the future of the activity. One or more of the team, be it small or large, needs to be interested in what goes on in the outside world. The team will continually access a host of sources—the Internet, newspapers, TV news and interviews, lectures, journals, books, conversations with experts—that will furnish candidate issues for the Big Externalities list. Typically included will be (1) government actions, budgets, and policies, from local to international; (2) science and technology breakthroughs in everything from information handling, health, and energy to food, education, travel, and amusement; (3) wars and natural disasters; (4) the environment, from local weather changes to Earth's warming; and (5) the world economy.

EXTERNALITIES AND PLANS

Forecasting the future for any activity goes hand-in-hand, of course, with planning for that activity. If a business plan calls for making a big acquisition or selling off a division or making a new entry into a foreign country, the activity's forecast is set in part by such plans just as it is partly determined by continuation of other activities. What the management desires for the future, tries to cause to take place, and hence needs to see described in the forecast may be impacted by Big Externalities. If all the experts predict much higher interest rates ahead, the leader of a business might need to consider postponing a previously planned plant expansion that was to be financed by a high level of borrowing.

A wealthy entrepreneur in India, let us imagine, is looking for American products to manufacture in India for the world market. At the same time, your small U.S. company in the home appliance business has a promising new idea for a radically different kind of microwave oven. You lack the capital to develop that new product and to finance a factory to manufacture it. It may then be sensible for you to seek financing from that Indian entrepreneur in a deal to design the product in the United States, manufacture it in India, and market it everywhere in the world. The plan and the forecast will evolve together.

Some conspicuous externalities can be immediately seen by you, the forecaster, as probably having little effect on the planning for your specialized activity. Let's say that North Korea tests a nuclear bomb. That action has immediate impact on the forecasts for some South Korean businesses and for the United States' Department of Defense. Meanwhile, you, a retailer in the United

States enjoying profitable sales of cashmere sweaters made in China, are unaffected. External issues routinely should be scanned quickly to try to catch some severe potential influence on your activity. In view of the complexity that stands in the way of accurate assessment, it is usually best, however, to ignore equally quickly those observed externalities where no important connection is seen to be likely. The gamble—namely, that you might miss perceiving, and will regret later not preparing for, a bad negative or a promising positive—may be worth taking. Thus, if you find that the increasing price of oil seems clearly a minor factor in the activity you happen to be involved in, you should spend little time on attempts to predict the future range of the price of oil. This is especially a wise step if the "experts" seem divided more or less equally about whether the average future oil price will rise or fall.

Consider, as another example, the much discussed immigration problems of the United States. If you are involved with agriculture in California and are forecasting the moneymaking potential of your business in the next few years, you will be aware that governmental action regarding immigration will constitute a Big Externality to you with the possibility of greatly influencing the availability and cost of labor in your industry. On the other hand, the immigration problem might continue to appear, as now, too tough for the politicians to handle. Good solutions to the immigration problem, as a result, are not being invented, and the subject is only ineffectively being pursued by government leaders who have many other problems they may believe deserve higher priority. So a possibility, perhaps the most likely one, is that nothing of importance will be tried at the federal level for years, but only at that level can anything substantive be done. Important as you know the U.S. government approaches are certain to be to the forecasting of revenues and profits in your field, agriculture, you may conclude that the probability of substantive government effort is so low that it may be excusable for you to delay introducing this externality into your forecasting at this time.

In summary, plan to use ranges when listing possibilities for the future influence of Big Externalities on the activity you are managing. Limit your efforts at prediction to those externalities whose effects seem most likely to impact your activity. Be willing to gamble on devoting less attention to those phenomena where you anticipate the least influence on your operations, where the experts differ most, and where it is extremely difficult even to set a range for the possibility.

Part Two | Future Possibilities

Chapter Seven | The Future Automobile

Part 2 of this book presents examples of the application of the procedures for creating useful predictions that were set forth in Part 1. To illustrate those methods, we have chosen possibilities that are purposely varied and imaginative but also realistic, as they would have to be to provide the demonstrations we seek.

It may appear to the reader that in offering these scenarios, we seek to engage in predicting world events in the decades ahead. But that is not the case. Instead—and we wish to emphasize this point—our intention is more prosaic. It is to illustrate how to accomplish intelligent forecasting so as to prepare better for, and enable the shaping of, the future. We have carefully selected the examples that follow to provide a variety of different combinations of the probabilities, timings, potential influences on the predictors' activities, and the abilities of the predictors to influence the future. In this chapter we consider a possible future automobile, one that provides an example of how to employ the

Four-Measures rating approach to advance from possibilities to predictions.

The best-selling automobile in the future world may be small compared with today's typical cars.[1] It may accommodate only two passengers and be optimized for application to around half of the transportation needs of the planet's city drivers—for going to and from work, running errands, shopping, and taking kids to school, and serving as a teenager's first car or a single-passenger taxi. It will cost less than $10,000, will average around 100 miles to the gallon, pollute the air hardly at all, have a top speed of 40 miles an hour, and not be intended for long trips or for traveling on U.S. freeways. It will never need brake lining replacements, and it will require no change in the fuel distribution systems now in existence.

Larger and faster cars will continue to be produced. (Often perhaps, and unlike today's pattern, the larger automobiles may be rented by city drivers when needed.) Since the small cars will take up much less space, more parallel lanes will become available on some city streets, thus speeding traffic, and more parking spaces will be available in existing parking lots that will be able to accommodate more cars.

Design approaches to reach 100 miles per gallon are presently available, each based on the autos' being small and limited in speed. One design embodiment might be as follows: The car is driven by a single electric motor on the rear axle. This motor is powered by an electric battery that is small because when that battery drops to a low charge, it is automatically brought up in charge by an electric generator in the car driven by a gasoline or diesel engine possessing a sole operating mode. That engine is either off or it is in operation at only full power output. When an internal combustion engine is required to provide for a range of operating conditions, as is true for cars now, it needs varying fuel-to-air mixtures and timings of combustion, and the resulting engine is relatively inefficient, and it pollutes greatly. In contrast, when every detail of engine design is optimized around a single operating mode, a very high efficiency and comparatively clean and complete combustion can be caused to take place.

If the brake pedal is pressed in this future car, that act will reverse the electric motor's magnetic field, thus turning that motor temporarily into an electric generator. The result will be that most of the energy used to bring the car up to its momentary speed is recovered as that speed is reduced and that energy is returned to the battery. When stopped, this auto's expending of energy is zero. There is no idling during bumper-to-bumper traffic stops or while waiting for the green light. (Some hybrid cars available today do this; it is a proven development.)

Where will these autos come from? The parts and the autos may be produced, assembled, and marketed virtually anywhere in the world with most fabrication probably originating in low-wage countries: China, India, Mexico, Brazil, Thailand, African states, and so on. The final products will be suitable for the personal transportation needs of the city populations in many countries, so strong local markets will exist for the locally manufactured products.

THE PLUG-IN

A second embodiment for the future car to supply the bulk of the world's city driving requirements is a small "plug-in" all-electric car.[2] The user would connect the car to an outlet at the home

garage to provide a nightly electric battery charge more than adequate for the typical next day's driving. The pattern of operation
might also include the availability of plug-in facilities in most
employee parking lots and also in the average commercial and
general city parking facility. Upon parking the car, the driver
would plug it into the adjacent outlet and then slide his or her
"electric charge" card through the slot provided; the driver would
then be billed for the electric charge received.

Importantly, the installation also would be designed to extract
energy from the car's battery should its charge at the moment
happen to be over a preset amount. The driver's account then
would be credited automatically for the energy thus transferred
into the city's electric power system. That supposes something
that may become common, namely, that the car battery will usually receive at home more energy at night than it will need the
following day. This procedure would lessen the requirement to
increase the generating capacity of the area's electricity supplier,
that power company's demand being lower at night than in the
daytime. (The energy collected at night would be sold at a lower
price than the energy collected during the daytime.)

IMPACT ON THE ECONOMY

If you are a managerial executive of an entity having no direct
relationship to the automotive industry, you might still be interested in the possibility described in the foregoing. This is because
what will happen in the future in the automotive field will have a
great effect on the world economy and on government and private
decision making. Almost whatever you are managing will be

affected, and you will want to consider appropriate action ahead of time. For example, the drop in the demand for gasoline will be great in the United States if these small electric-petroleum hybrid cars replace larger gas-guzzler cars. Thus, the price of oil will decrease or increase more slowly. If people spend less on their personal transport needs, they will have money available for other things. If cars of small size proliferate, there will be more efficient use of real estate for parking. If there is less air pollution in our cities originating from our autos, city life will be healthier, and less funding may be needed for medical care.

RATING THE POSSIBILITY

Let us now rate this small electric car possibility as a step toward arriving at a useful forecast. We shall do so for an assumed American automotive parts marketer who has manufacturing plants in several countries. The Four Measures of this future possibility will be considered: (A) the probability of the possibility's actual occurrence; (B) the timing, if it happens; (C) the impact on this auto parts manufacturer's endeavors; and (D) the potential capability of that producer's acting early so as to shape its future.

We start with (A), the probability. It looks very likely. On a 1-to-10 basis, let us assign a 9 to the probability that half the personal cars of the world will be as described. When? For the (B) measure, let us estimate that the trend will be established in a few years and that the small cars described will be very common in 10 years. That suggests a figure of about 8 for (B). The impact (C) on the auto parts business will be huge because all the parts will have to be specially designed for these quite different cars.

This suggests a 9 for (C). Can the parts manufacturer act ahead to profit from reaching a high production rate for these small cars? Certainly much can be done: deals to be the supplier of parts with the companies that will be potential assemblers and marketers of the new cars, highly cooperative engineering design efforts with those companies, and optimum locating of new manufacturing plants internationally. (D) merits a 10.

In summary:

A. Probability	9
B. Timing	8
C. Impact	9
D. Action potential	10
Total	36

The total score for this possibility is high, so consideration of this possibility's becoming a prediction deserves a high priority. Chances are that few other possibilities will equal or exceed this rating for a typical U.S.-based auto parts producer, so it should declare this possibility to be a prediction and act on it, all out, starting immediately.

But what if you, the forecaster, turn out to be wrong? As recommended in Part 1 of this book, you must examine what the consequences to you might be if the bulk of your future business has been planned around the described future automobile and it does not happen. Before you commit to action on this possibility, as you turn it into a prediction, you must answer these questions: How big a loss might you incur? What might you do to minimize that loss as you are forced to redo your forecast for the future?

Chapter Eight | Terrorism in the United States

Destruction of the World Trade Center Towers in New York City was a terrible disaster. Why did Osama bin Laden kill 3,000 Americans that day? According to some it was because he had not yet perfected the means to kill 300,000. Potential future terrorist acts could be vastly more penalizing in every dimension of tragedy and of overall economic and societal impairment of the United States.

In this chapter we shall consider possibilities of such terrorism. The expertise and training needed by terrorists who might perform every item in the following compilation are modest, and the materials and apparatus required are readily available in the United States. In fact, the entire group of events about to be described—that would leave America in horrible chaos—could all be accomplished in as few as 100 continuous days by a team of only 100 terrorists. Such difficult-to-prevent and violent terrorism would be entirely practical for terrorists to carry out. It is accordingly a serious possibility.

100 ACTS/100 DAYS

- In New York's subways, timed to the morning rush hour, powerful explosives in very small packages, set to go off in 30 minutes, are left in 100 different trains. (The 100 terrorists leave ahead of the programmed explosions; they do not commit suicide and instead are immediately available for a next task.) Going far beyond the subway and surface train terrorism that occurred in Tokyo, London, and Madrid a few years back—by virtue of superior planning and execution—thousands of passengers would be killed. The damage would be at the level of hundreds of billions of dollars, and New York City's operations would be severely handicapped for a long period as would be many operations elsewhere in the nation that are intertwined with New York City's.

- Something similar is performed the next day on U.S. passenger and freight trains.

- The following day telephone central stations in 100 cities are bombed simultaneously.

- Ditto, police and fire stations in large cities.

- Ditto, TV and radio stations.

- Ditto, chemical plants and gasoline storage areas.

- Ditto, electric power generation and transmission facilities.

- Ditto, water supply and waste treatment centers.

- Ditto, hospitals.

- Ditto, dams.

- Ditto, government office buildings.

- Ditto, the public access areas of major airline terminals.

- Ditto, the public access areas of large city bus stations.

- Ditto, 100 railroad tank cars that are loaded with chlorine and other toxic chemicals and are momentarily in transit in populated areas.
- Ditto, anthrax is distributed in an aerosol attack in 100 U.S. cities.

This incomplete list, unpleasant as it is to contemplate, is far from the total of possibilities that could be imagined in this easy-for-the-terrorists category. Does anyone really believe that 100 terrorists would have great difficulty in making entry into the United States carrying no apparatus or materials and that they could not acquire the apparatus and materials they would need within the United States?

THE CONSEQUENCES

If the just described terrorist campaign actually were to take place, the U.S. response would be to make fighting this new terrorism the nation's top priority. In addition to National Guard and state militias being called out, volunteer forces would be organized to watch over a large number of the nation's remaining key facilities in every community.

After the long time period required to bring the New York subway system back to operation, the Department of Homeland Security (DHS) would station observers on each and every subway train in New York, passengers and their packages would be scanned, and the subway cars would be equipped in great detail with cameras and other observing and sensing equipment and with radio transmitters in constant communication with new command stations. The same would be installed for numerous facilities all over the country. Like commercial airlines, railroad passenger trains would incorporate passenger and baggage searches before allowing entry. The Congress would quickly pass high budgets for the FBI, the CIA, the DHS, the DoD, and all other national government agencies involved in controlling entry and movement of individuals, equipment, and materials into and about the United States. Increased funding would be made available to police and fire departments. Every U.S. land, sea, and air entry port, all major facilities, and every concentration of people and assets in the land would now be seen as candidates for further terrorist acts. Surveillance of the population would be stepped up dramatically, and traditional American privacy laws and practice would be altered.

Anticipation of further terrorism in the United States after 9/11 caused the establishment of the Cabinet-level Department of Homeland Security (DHS). It would be greatly expanded after the described 100 days' attacks because the U.S. government would attempt the prior discovery and prevention of such terrorism. Efforts would be made to imagine what plans terrorists might consider as they prepare to hit more American targets, and counteractions would be prepared. What additional terrorist plots are conceivable? What would the terrorists need in order to carry out each such plot? What would be the timing? What conceivable evidence might be uncovered regarding the terrorists' planning? To support such expanded analytical information-handling duties for the DHS, a huge new computerized data system would be set up, itself a candidate for terrorist targeting. The American standard of living would drop severely to pay for all this expanded security activity.

THE U.S. INFORMATION SYSTEMS AS A TARGET

The recently created DHS system would not be the only information system of interest to terrorists. America's critical infrastructure is based heavily on information networking, from our electric power distribution system to the Internet, from voice communications to airline control, from banking to manufacturing. The possibility would have to be considered that disastrous terrorism will be attempted in the future by highly technically trained and well-financed personnel who would find the U.S. IT infrastructure an irresistible target. A well-planned, high-technology, computer-based attack on the United States' IT installations could bring a large fraction of the nation's operations to a halt. (An attack in fact was apparently conducted against the information infrastructure of Estonia in 2007.) By causing a loss of computer-based data, the terrorists would hope to generally disrupt the U.S. economy and impair the nation's ability to respond to any kind of terrorist attack.

To counter such attacks, the following specific questions would need answers:

- What exactly might IT terrorists seek to do in the future to America's IT infrastructure? Make critical systems inoperative? Steal secret access codes? Plant false information?
- What should the United States do to upgrade the nation's IT infrastructure to resist those possible IT terrorism attacks and ensure that America's IT systems will survive and be available to response agencies in the United States before, during, and after terrorism acts of all kinds?[1]
- How can the United States detect and counter terrorist attacks on its IT infrastructure before they happen?

If you are the manager of a factory or hospital or service organization or any business, the possibility of IT terrorism suggests you should ponder what you can do to ensure your own information units will survive and enable your continued operation. Even a mere listing of possibilities for evil computer operations experts to create chaos in the data storage and processing systems basic to all of America's activities would require a large team of information technology specialists.

WORSE TERRORISM POSSIBILITIES

Unfortunately, as a later chapter in this book describes, the DHS must also deal with the fact that dangerous nuclear and biochemical equipment and matter will be in the hands of terrorist groups with available funds (or merely the right credentials as judged by the possessors and willing transferers of the capability). The DHS information system will need to attempt to monitor the world's accumulation of dangerous material and apparatus. Where in the world specifically is this inventory held, and where might it be moving? Who are the active experts around the world who might sell their expertise?

Our concerns do not need to go all the way to the terrorists' possible employment of the most modern, advanced, megaton hydrogen bombs—single weapons that could each kill tens of millions—in order to take seriously a broadened nuclear terrorism danger well beyond the list earlier presented.[2]

Consider the following examples:

- Non-nuclear bombs are tossed (at night, by a simple device from a passing truck) at U.S. nuclear waste storage areas, thereby causing the spewing of dangerous radioactive matter into the atmosphere and forcing the abandonment of large populated areas.

- Devices that spray into the air germs of a death-causing disease are placed simultaneously in many occupied sports arenas.
- Letters containing extremely poisonous powder are mailed to offices and homes of thousands of U.S. local government leaders.
- Radioactive material is now routinely stored loosely in hospitals, universities, and factories. A stick of cobalt is easily stolen from a food irradiation plant, and such a stick can be blown up with a pound of explosive. An assembly of "dirty bombs" could contaminate a major city with much of the population made seriously ill. Millions of people might have to be denied access to several contaminated cities for years.

Terrorists planning to use nuclear bombs or deadly biochemical weapons in America might assemble those items here from imported pieces. Seeking evidence of preparation of such potential terrorism clearly would have to be on an international scale. The DHS's information system would have to operate everywhere. That the United States will decide it must endeavor to create such an international effort must be considered a possibility.

RATING THE POSSIBILITY

The catastrophes inherent in the terrorism possibilities we have described suggest that we need to assume the issue will interest the White House. Imagine we are advisors to the president who consults us regarding this matter. How do we proceed? Let us start with the Four Measures, even though we sense that as to this possibility, the numeric ratings will at most be a guide.

Because it appears so easy for terrorists to prepare for and accomplish many of the acts we have listed, and because the effects on the United States would be so penalizing, we must choose the figure 10 for (A), the probability of its occurring. Because such attacks can be carried out soon after terrorists have decided to proceed with them, we are forced also to assign a 10—that is, soon, only years away, not decades—for (B), the timing. The impact (C) would be horrible, thus calling again for a 10. Next, what can the United States do ahead of time after taking the prediction seriously? The answer is, take a considerable number of precautions; yet unfortunately, such precautions are so speculative that we must choose a mere 2 for (D).[3]

In summary:

A. Probability	10
B. Timing	10
C. Impact	10
D. Action potential	2
Total	32

This total score is not extremely high because of the low (D), yet the president must act as if the possibility is a certain prediction! He or she has no choice in view of the size of the disaster should it happen.

What if the prediction turns out wrong? In this case that fortunately would be all to the good.

Let us imagine the Four-Measures procedure is applied by a rather different predictor than the president—namely, the leader of a defense company that is a major contractor for U.S. government information systems. The measures (A), (B), and (C) would appear to remain at 10 for this specific rater. The probability is high, the time soon, and the effect on the corporation's future also the highest because the possibility of this kind of terrorism equates to the highest priority for U.S. government action that ensures large government contracts. That means (D) is now also high because this company, if alert in its field, will quickly prepare for the government's demand for new, complex, and expensive security systems (even if their adequacy will not make America completely safe). The U.S. president and Congress will have no choice but to budget for doing whatever is likely to reduce the probability that the terrorists' efforts will succeed.

So this defense company's leader will assign to (D) an 8, yielding a final score of 38, which is very high. That company should speedily work on writing and submitting proposals to the U.S. government, turning this possibility into a prediction item for its future, which it will endeavor to shape.

Chapter Nine | China and the Asian Military Arena

What China is becoming will impact greatly the future of America.[1] In this chapter we describe China-based issues that might particularly affect plans of the U.S. Department of Defense (DoD). In military preparedness the DoD has been known to fail to act early sometimes on a coming threat to the nation that calls for highly innovative developments. One possibility that may not be receiving the effort it deserves stems from potential rivalry between the United States and China for superiority in the East Asian oceans and the air and space above them.[2] Some highly respected analysts predict that the United States will retain its general military superiority over China for the foreseeable future.[3] Even if true, more creative conceptual thinking and implementations may be needed in diplomacy with China.

China may be thought of as made up of two parts: The first is a coastal entity of roughly 200 million population that is developing rapidly.[4] It is tied to a second, inland China. The first China has already reached a level of industrialization, science and technology capabilities, and military potency that in many respects is in the class of Japan, Germany, Britain, France, and Russia. In some aspects coastal China already today rates higher than those nations. The second and inland China is highly undeveloped, yet it is not a handicap to coastal China because it provides accessible natural resources and it is a huge potential labor pool. China does not need to import workers as do the United States and Western Europe, and it can readily maintain a huge land army.

CHINA, ECONOMIC GIANT

No military threat from China can be considered sensibly without also studying China's future as an economic giant, one growing at a rate of nearly 10 percent per year and holding a trillion dollars of foreign currency. Today's GNP per capita in China is more than 10 times what it was two decades ago.[5] China possesses strong high-technology competence in electronics, missiles, spacecraft, nucleonics, and manufacturing. In these areas, in one more decade China will likely surpass Japan, every European country, and Russia. By 2050 China is projected to have about 1.5 billion people, nearly four times the 400 million inhabitants projected for the United States. If China were to achieve one half the per capita income of the United States by the middle of this century, its economy would be twice the size of the U.S. economy.[6]

In the early years of this century, the economic growth in China has constituted over 15 percent of the total world economy's growth. China has encouraged other countries to invest in China, which they have done to a total of roughly half a trillion dollars. China's policies are aggressively geared to the goal of increased trade with the developed world as China expands quickly from being only a mass supplier of low-cost labor on nontechnological products (such as clothes) to large-scale manufacture of the most complex of industrial equipment and the most sophisticated of electronics gear.[7] China's universities graduate about half a million engineers a year, five times the U.S. output. China is a big exporter of DVD players and digital cameras, its low-priced labor being dominant in these areas. China has over 400 million fixed phone lines, and in 2007 over 150 million Chinese used the Internet, a quarter of them accessing it through their cell phones. Over 200 million Chinese enjoy cable TV—more than the number of Americans—and China leads the world in cell phone users, which is expected to approach a billion by 2015.

UNITED STATES–CHINA COOPERATION

It is critical to the growth of the Chinese economy that relations with the United States be friendly. Trade between the two countries is growing rapidly. U.S. imports from China, around $250 billion in 2006, doubled in the previous five years. U.S. shipments to China were at $50 billion in 2006, tripling the rate of five years earlier. Despite political scars over the outsourcing of manufacturing, those benefiting most in the United States from this trade have been low-income Americans who have gained access to consumer goods they could not previously afford. Meanwhile U.S. manufacturers' international sales are rising in part due to the outsourcing to China that has enabled U.S. companies to be more competitive against foreign manufacturers.

Accordingly, we must consider it a possibility that China might be a more than willing contributor to world stability, a cooperative partner to the United States, rather than a military threat. There are, however, other possibilities. Some patterns of potential future behavior by China are less compatible with world stability as the United States will judge it. Examples follow.

CHINA, MILITARY GIANT

China is not today a conventional sea power. The U.S. Navy, in effect, protects the ocean lanes needed for bringing oil and other vital supplies to China. We should not be surprised if China, in the not distant future, becomes independently confident of deliveries to it by ocean by building up its own navy. It is known to have underway today a major naval ship-building program.

China is a nuclear power, and it has an unresolved difference with another nuclear power, the United States, over the status of Taiwan. We must list as a possibility that China will plan and act so as to possess the capability to take over Taiwan—indeed, to succeed in doing so should it decide on that course even if the United States should forcibly resist it. Taiwan's rapidly growing industry, with very considerable U.S. financing and ties, has moved much of its large-scale technological product manufacturing to China. Taiwan leads in investment there with amounts well over the hundred billion dollar level. Thus the leaders of China, the United States, and Taiwan certainly have reason to prefer not to engage in a war stemming from Taiwan's announcing its independence. But if Taiwan were to do that, China might have no choice but to forcibly invade that island, and the United States might feel it must support Taiwan in resisting the takeover.

What would China build as a takeover military force? What must the DoD do to prepare the United States to oppose successfully any attempt by China to take over Taiwan? What in the way of ships, missiles, spacecraft, and so on, is it possible that China, Taiwan, and the United States will each believe it must possess? Could some new U.S. force play havoc with a Chinese invasion force headed for Taiwan? Would perhaps the United States' implementing such a system cause China to reject invasion in favor of peaceful alternatives regarding Taiwan?

CHINA'S R&D EFFORTS

It is a strong possibility that China will plan to be a high-tech power in utilizing space. It may plan to interfere with the United States' space-based equipment if it sees it as used too aggressively to observe China's activities. Indeed, China's destruction of an older satellite of its own in early 2007 sent a strong signal of capability and potential intent. China will not expect to become, as has the United States, a victim of terrorism, and thus it will not be required to assign a high priority to possessing the ability to fight it. China then might not feel the need, as does the United States, to create and maintain a global spaced-based system for collecting information concerning potential actions of terrorists and rogue nations. Yet China's ambition to reach top military readiness status on a broad scale is serious and might push China into some activities the United States will regard as unnecessary. (This can be said, after all, even about China's having become a nuclear power.) China's determination to be regarded as a leader in military technology clearly arises in great part from a psychological, prestige-seeking base. China wants to be respected as a powerful nation technologically, possessing high stature in both civilian and military technology.

So China will become increasingly strong militarily and will engage in a significant R&D effort to develop advanced weapons systems. The United States will have no choice but to keep China's military activities under detailed watch because the United States cannot allow a surprising technology breakthrough by China to upset the environment affecting war and peace.

CHINA'S SPACE AMBITIONS

China has grabbed the lead as the supplier (also the principal financial sponsor) of satellites to undeveloped countries. It has built and launched or it is the contractor for future satellites for various commercial purposes for such countries as Venezuela, Pakistan, Nigeria, and Bangladesh. To these nations, satellites are status symbols, and, for China, supplying them is a way of locking up deals for oil and other resources and for gaining membership in the high-tech information technology world. The countries possessing these Chinese satellites sell bandwidth to other of the world's users. Satellites enable their owners to monitor their oil pipelines and enable them to deliver educational programs to TV sets in the more remote parts of their countries. The space satellite business offers an attractive way for China to invest its huge currency reserves. It has been estimated that China will launch over 100 satellites in the next decade.

Of course, China also will assign a high priority to placing unmanned equipment in space to enable observation of all conceivable activities by any nation in China's regions of land, ocean, air, and space. Such means for China might be accompanied by its also developing ways to counter the United States' possessing the power to take out China's space apparatus. Each nation might prepare to win should space warfare break out.[8]

China's apparent efforts in both unmanned and manned spacecraft already exceed Russian and European efforts. China might come to be seen in the future as a more sensible partner for the United States than Russia for such projects as future manned stations in space or on the Moon, or even for eventually landing human beings on Mars. (Of course, that planet might come to be seen in the United States as adequately and more sensibly explorable by unmanned instrument packages. Mars and lunar landings by Americans might then be ruled out as extremely expensive, life-endangering, and virtually worthless projects. But there continue to be advocates for ongoing American person-in-space programs for various psychological reasons, for example, "inspiring our young people." The United States' cooperating with China on such programs, if they must exist, might turn out to be a sensible course of action for both countries.)

China is doubtless studying the U.S. person-in-space program[9]— that is, "we shall return to the Moon and use it as a base to send astronauts to land on Mars"—with no realistic commitment to fund it.[10] China might conclude it has an opportunity to take over first place in placing humans in space. We should not be astonished if China announces a plan to establish a permanent base on the Moon and also to seek credibility about its sending an astronaut to Mars before we do. Of course, China's military leaders know that a person-in-space program will not yield military advantages, but a beneficial psychological side-effect would be adequate justification to China for its development. China might hope to use that program to acquire world respect—just as the USSR did with its *Sputnik* and cosmonauts. China doubtless aspires to be second to no other nation in mass production of many advanced technology products to meet the world's commercial, nonmilitary needs, and it might believe it could reach that position more directly if it also attained enhanced standing for its space programs.

THE FUTURE U.S. ASIAN NAVY

China might be in a class by itself as a candidate partner for the United States' future attempts at solving world problems through diplomacy. More specifically, where China and the United States might differ on any problem, predictors should include the possibility that economic factors might outweigh military-based ones as the two countries hunt for solutions, at times doing so jointly.

Meanwhile, as evidence of a possible lack of adequate predictive vision, the DoD has indicated that recent high annual expenditures for U.S. Navy ships may not continue. Of course, the DoD may well not need many more ships of the kind it has been buying. Indeed, a competent examination of the future race between China and the United States for superiority in the East

Asian waters might result in determining that the future U.S. Navy force stationed there should be somewhat different from the present one. An alternative need for the future—to speculate to make a point and list a possibility—might conceivably turn out to be for mass-produced, small, superfast ships, each carrying ready-to-launch unmanned air vehicles (UAVs) and ballistic missiles, with each of these ships also unmanned and controlled via space satellites.

THE PROBLEM OF NORTH KOREA

The actions of China, Taiwan, the two Koreas, Japan, and Russia will all participate in defining future U.S. military requirements in East Asia. Consider, for example, the problem of North Korea's possessing nuclear bomb capability. The United States' concerns about North and South Korea must include the possibility of war between them and our consequent involvement. This is one reason we must worry about North Korea's potential nuclear weapons capability. China, however, which supplies North Korea with food, energy, and other necessities, is far more capable of influencing North Korea than is the United States.

It would be insane for that rogue nation's dictator to direct a nuclear bomb at America, but we have to include the possibility that he may act crazily. Indeed, North Korean missile tests are demonstrating longer and longer ranges. The Chinese may see it differently. It is possible they do not believe the North Korean dictator is insane, and should they come to believe he is, they would plan to eliminate him quickly. In any case, China will want to be the "decider"—not let the United States have that role—about anything related to either Korea.[11] It might, for example, please China if the two Koreas would join to become one nation, but only as one closely cooperative with China in all matters. It is a likely possibility that highly cooperative diplomatic efforts by the United States with China might be far preferable to our participating in arms racing with China in East Asia's waters and the space above it.[12]

JAPAN AND RUSSIA

What about Japan's and Russia's Asian interests? Can we expect Japan to accept being a poor third and ceding control of the East Asian waters to China and the United States? Japan currently is, and is likely to remain, a long-term military ally of the United States in Asia, but the United States and Japan are competitors in important nonmilitary respects. As to security, the two nations are not to be expected always to see eye to eye. Japan's ideas about security are bound to differ importantly from America's if for no other reason than that historically the Chinese really hate the Japanese but not the Americans.

Russia might be forced to give East Asia less priority than other areas that it may have to rate as more important. But Russia is there permanently, and its presence cannot be ignored; perhaps Russia might be helpful to the United States in diplomacy with China. In fact, a China–United States–Russia–Japan long-term peaceful cooperation for solving all East Asia security problems is not to be ruled out as a possibility, even as China and the United States are competitors for military superiority there.

Never in history have the two most powerful nations of the world been in the position of needing to prepare for being military enemies and yet fated simultaneously to be locked into an ever-tightening involvement with each other in their peacetime endeavors. China's vital economic strength, growth, and stability are extremely dependent on U.S. trade. China needs continued huge exports to the United States. In time China's leaders will feel the pressure to do more with their growing pile of U.S. government bonds than simply collect interest payments. They likely will be a large acquirer of various U.S.-based assets.[13] America's economic strength and policies will become increasingly affected by what happens in China and by each nation's being a major investor in the other.

RATING THE POSSIBILITY

Predicting by the United States' DoD must be a routine procedure as regards China. First, the DoD must list possibilities, some of which have been described in the foregoing. Then, the Four Measures presented in Chapter 3 should be applied for refining the list: (A) probability of occurrence, (B) time of occurrence, (C) severity of impact if the possibility should become a reality, and (D) ability to influence the future to improve it by early action.

What of the other aspects of American life? How does China affect the U.S. manufacturers of commercial apparatus, our universities, producers of clothing, furniture, agricultural equipment, and food? How should American companies handle the Big Externalities originating from China that will have an important impact on forecasting and shaping their futures? Some consequences seem easy to predict. Outsourcing manufacturing to China will increasingly be planned by American producers.

Cooperative arrangements for financing Chinese manufacturing will be made by American financing companies. American companies will set up many subsidiaries in China. China will buy large and small American companies. Venture capital firms will be established in China with help from and in partnership with American venture capital companies. These are all important possibilities.

Let us choose one possibility, namely, a war over Taiwan, for illustrating further the application of the Four-Measures rating: First, (A), how likely (1 to 10) is it that the United States will find itself at war with China over Taiwan? We submit that it is improbable that such a war will occur. If it does, it will be far off in time (B), when conceivably the present situation might change for unforeseen reasons. This is because Taiwan-China trade is so huge and of very high importance to each. Taiwan, triggering this war by announcing to the world that it is an independent nation and asking for separate membership in the United Nations, would severely endanger its investment in and trade with China (now in the hundreds of billions of dollars) and would lower its economic status. It would virtually stop its economic growth because its military expenditures would have to rise enormously. The impact (C) on the DoD would be high because influential sources would see promises by the United States to defend Taiwan as having to be kept.

Could the United States take actions ahead of time to affect the results (D)? The answer is yes. Changing U.S. policy and allowing China's takeover of Taiwan is conceivable. Enormous diplomatic efforts on relationships with both China and Taiwan to avoid all war-fostering actions might be the U.S. reaction.

The United States' influence on both China and Taiwan (D) could be very powerful because of the importance of trade, investment, and technology transfer to and from the United States to both China and Taiwan.

In summary:

A. Probability	2
B. Timing	2
C. Impact	9
D. Action potential	8
Total	21

This total suggests that a war with China over Taiwan may not be the most likely future for which the DoD ought to prepare. But what if such a prediction turns out to be wrong? The consequences might not necessarily be great for the United States. If the DoD is caught unprepared to defend Taiwan against a sudden, surprising, well-prepared Chinese attack, and we are accordingly forced to allow that island's takeover by China, it would be an embarrassment; but it need not lead to a war between two nuclear powers that might spiral with unintended consequences. Most U.S. citizens might view Taiwan as not our fight and might react to it the same way the British public handled the changeover with apparent ease when Hong Kong became part of China.

Chapter Ten | K-12 Education in the United States

Every time U.S. public schooling is compared with that of other developed countries through common testing, it receives extremely bad ratings. This is true for reading and writing skills, mathematics, science, foreign languages, and the fraction of students entering high school who graduate. Fear is growing that if the priority is not raised on improving primary and secondary education in America, the nation's economy, security, and standard of living will suffer greatly. U.S. citizens are now demanding that something effective be done about this highly negative situation. Thus, it is reasonable to list the possibility that in the future the desire for action will impact the political process importantly with candidates for office favored when seen as truly determined and competent on the education front.

But what specifically might happen? We have claimed in this text that the first step in useful predicting is to list possibilities and be imaginative in doing so, thus to increase the chances that all important eventualities are surfaced. It is not the purpose of this chapter to offer our predictions of what will happen to U.S. education in the future. We simply present in this chapter one possibility, a conceivable future development that will illustrate further the Four-Measures approach to rating possibilities. Specifically, we consider the application of advanced technology to the education process. We shall describe a major change in the role of the teacher, the creation of a new education industry, and the coming of new professions in the field of high school education.

A New System

In the following imagined future high school, upon registering, each student will receive an identity card and a personal identification number (PIN). The card or the PIN is introduced by the student each morning into a special machine located in the school's entry hall. This computer-based unit is connected to a data system that enables it to print out information so that the student will know where to go at various times of that day. A typical school day will consist of a number of sessions, some of which will take place, as now, in rooms with other students and a teacher. The rest of the school day will involve various teaching machines.

Can hyperactive and attention-deficit high school students be expected to sit for hours before a machine? A good question at the outset. Young people actually do exactly that if the machine is a TV set. Many can do so in front of a computer whose games—and the communication capabilities with friends and strangers that machine makes possible—can be irresistible.

It might be argued at the outset that attempts to enhance or replace any portion of the teaching staff's duties with electronic aids would have at least one very fundamental limitation. Without a highly intelligent and experienced teacher present, we might well fear that any system presenting matter to students by use of machinery will miss the necessary judging of the student's understanding of the presentation. What is presented will not be adjustable to the students' needs because that requires hearing the students' questions and responses. It requires also recognizing and nipping weaknesses and misunderstandings in the bud and generally providing the interactions between teacher and student essential to successful learning. Of course, we can readily introduce videos to partially replace a lecturer, and we can invent apparatus intended to make more efficient the use of a skilled teacher's time. But we presumably should expect to use even the most effective teaching machines only for a limited fraction of the total school day.

In the possible systems about to be described, modern technology is applied so as to eliminate this apparently fundamental limitation. One objective of everything pictured in the following is to raise teachers to a higher level in their contributions to the teaching process by removing from their duties those portions which do not use the teachers' skills to the fullest and that can be delivered more effectively by machines.

A TRIGONOMETRY COURSE

We illustrate by imagining a student registered for a high school course in trigonometry. She will spend several hours a week learning this branch of math mainly in automated classrooms. A presentation machine will provide basic concepts in trigonometry to students in a classroom by lectures delivered through a motion picture. In such a film, human teachers will be shown narrating trigonometry principles to the accompaniment of animated geometrical diagrams. Each classroom chair will include a set of push buttons, and the student will insert her identification card in the provided slot. That act will automatically record her presence and will connect her button pushing to a "master" record-keeping machine. Throughout the presentation the student will be called upon to respond to questions. She will be asked about the material just presented in the form of multiple choices, and the system will record her choices. She will be informed by the lights on the arm of her chair whether her answers are correct or wrong.

The trigonometry concept being offered at any time may be repeated automatically if too many of the class are found not to grasp it the first time, and then more questions will be asked. The student may be asked to indicate whether she thinks she understands what is being presented and whether she wishes it were slower or faster. If most students seem not to understand the presentation, the machine will shift to an alternative, perhaps slower, presentation. The student will be in constant communication with a computer that controls presentation speed and alternatives. The student's responses will be recorded, processed, and used by the electronic master analyzing and scheduling system as it chooses next steps throughout the presentation.

Another approach will be for the student to sit alone in front of a machine, again with an animated video presentation and a keyboard. The programming system will automatically select from its file the appropriate presentations for that particular student—that is, it is ready to go fast if that student's record so suggests or slow if that student's progress has proved slow. As this machine presents trigonometry principles, it will ask for responses to determine that student's progress. Based upon the student's answers, it may repeat a presentation or go on to the next step or even skip steps. It will repeat what the student has missed earlier and will gloss over what she has proven she knows well. This machine is prepared to take a single principle and go over it many times if necessary, altering the presentation perhaps with additional detail, maybe trying another way of looking at it, always hoping to succeed in obtaining from the individual student before it the responses indicating that the principle being presented is well enough understood so that the machine should go on to the next step. A brilliant student could race through the trigonometry course in a small fraction of the usual time. A slower student would have to spend more time with the machine.

THE FEEDBACK CONCEPT

The teaching machines and the subject matter, we observe, are all tied to the students in a feedback relationship. Admittedly, this machine system will not cover all that an excellent human trigonometry teacher, one focused on that one pupil, might observe and act on. It will provide, however, a good portion of what that teacher might accomplish because the machine system will offer a very efficient and dynamically interesting and varied (and tailored to that one student) presentation of most of the required basic material, and, at the same time, it will deliver a useful record, one enabling study of the student's progress in understanding trigonometry. Of course, before a very bright student is deemed to have mastered trigonometry unusually speedily, a session with that student conducted by a skilled human teacher might be a good idea. That teacher will be aided by having before him the student's record of what could be many periods of intensive machine-student interfacings.

Some students will learn better than others with these machines. With records readily available in the system, system developers will be able to judge in what way the operation is inadequate and needs to be altered or supplemented. With proper cooperation among experts in teaching, trigonometry, and machine and system engineering, these systems will evolve so as to realize the maximum of benefits.

In addition to potentially improving student learning, teachers might benefit as well. Using electronic machines to provide routine instruction and feedback to large numbers of students frees up the (fewer number of) teachers to focus on the more creative and rewarding aspects of their jobs. This could provide the nation with a smaller number of more highly motivated (and better compensated) educators.

MEMORIZING MACHINES

Let us illustrate these concepts further by some quite different examples. Consider "memorizing machines" (some forms of which are already in use). Facility in some subjects requires that certain information be readily available to the mind—like the weights of the chemical elements when studying chemistry. But what a drudgery it is to memorize them. Memorizing machines can remove much boredom and make memorizing efficient and fun. For instance, the machine can call out the chemical elements, with the student's responding by punching in the corresponding atomic weights on a keyboard. When he errs, not only does a red light flash but the machine also displays the correct answer and it remembers that he has missed it. As the machine continues to chase through the list, it again names some of the elements that the student has already answered correctly, just to be sure, and to give him useful repetitive exercise; it comes back frequently to those chemical elements where he gave the wrong answer earlier. Minutes a day spent with memorizing machines can accomplish more for the student than much more time spent memorizing in other ways.

ENGLISH AND BEYOND

The above described machine-based teaching and studying methods might require such concentration by the student that they would not be practical to use for the entire school day. But before we discuss such limitations, and before we elaborate on the fundamental differences that this kind of technological development could bring to the education process, let us consider one or two more examples.

The use of machines in which the student and the presentation are in responsive communication might be helpful in the study of basic concepts in science and mathematics, in the learning of principles, and in the acquisition of facts. But what about such things as English composition or the study of foreign languages? Teaching English is difficult, as is instilling into students an appreciation of good literature. But even here teaching machines and their software programs are readily conceivable that will efficiently expose students to the tools of good reading, writing, and speaking. We can elect to leave the more difficult aspects—the artistic and creative use of vocabulary and phrasing when writing, for example—for sessions of students with skilled teachers. Again, this serves to enrich the work content and heighten the motivation of a smaller number of dedicated teachers.

Mastering foreign languages involves considerable memorization. Memorizing machines might well have their place in vocabulary building. Grammar instruction is in great part the learning of rules. Machine presentations of such rules, with students' responding to questions presenting right and wrong alternatives, are easily imagined. Even audio presentations and recordings of experts' versus students' pronunciations could be offered by the machines for aid in learning the proper speaking of foreign languages. More complex aspects of teaching the reading and speaking of foreign languages could be left for human teachers. Their rise to a higher intellectual level of language education would be made possible and practical in part because the machines would provide the mechanical, the lower intellectual level, of language education.

THE REQUIRED RESOURCES

What resources would this future high school have to possess? To begin with, the physical plant would need to include much apparatus that does not now exist but that can be designed and constructed with today's level of art and technology. A large technology-based new industry would be needed for the creating of the hardware and software, both for the presentations and for the data processing and analysis of student responses by the machines. A new profession, *education engineering*, would come into existence. The industrial organizations concerned with producing the specific needs for the teaching of mathematics, for example, would have to employ experts in education, mathematics, and engineering. Those experts would have to be in steady contact with the skilled teachers making up the high school staff so as to improve the system. New teaching specialists would have to be developed and employed to study and evaluate the various ways of designing and using the machine system.

Need we be concerned that with this kind of educational system students might suffer from dealing much of the time with cold machines in place of warm human teachers? Conceivably. But perhaps no more than when they read books by themselves, instead of always listening in a classroom to an oral presentation by a human teacher or spending hours a day in front of their personal computers.

MIGHT IT HAPPEN?

Is this high-tech education system likely to actually eventuate? Alas, the economics, school district bureaucracy, and potential teachers' union problems make that doubtful. Unless most trigonometry students in the United States use the same software and hardware, the costs of teaching trigonometry by the system described would be huge. The possibility of the broad utilization of the imagined new technology for transforming K-12 education in the United States would appear to require that the U.S. government be the sponsor, that being the only way to imagine widespread mass application to bring the costs down. The United States, in other words, would essentially have to adopt a "standard, national curriculum." That is common in other countries, but it is contrary to American tradition and the United States's separate state and local powers. Also, we could expect difficult teachers' union problems. All this implies complexity of organization and operation and much delay arising from the associated politics of national government decision making and funding.

Radically new ways to educate in the K-12 years based on technological advance are certainly technologically feasible. But is such advance politically realistic? Should it be considered for the predictor's list? It may deserve being rated a possibility but only a long-term one. But perhaps any major improvement of K-12 education in the United States by any conceivable means is at best a long-term possibility.

RATING THE POSSIBILITY

Let us now assume that we are engaged in predictions for the leader of a high-tech company seeking new product areas. Should the leader of that company invest R&D funds to develop the systems described, hardware and software, with the likelihood of generating profits from installing and operating the systems in American schools?

From the foregoing discussion, we propose the following ratings:

1. *Probability that business success will occur?* Rather low, a 2.

2. *Timing.* If it happens, it will be because the general idea will come to be seen as making so much sense that some form and degree of development, installation, and realization will eventually result. But bringing it about will take many years. For (B) we suggest again a 2.

3. *Impact if it happens.* We submit that the consequences of bold and broad use of high tech to improve teaching would be enormous. But the financial return on private corporation investment will be very low no matter how brilliant and perfect the designs and how tireless the marketing; (C) is also a 2.

4. *Can we act early to make it happen so as to profit when it does?* The answer is close to zero. Call it 1.

In summary:

A. Probability	2
B. Timing	2
C. Impact	2
D. Action potential	1
Total	7

This possibility is not one that should become a prediction for a well-managed high-tech company. But let us alter the possibility a bit. Suppose that instead of the entire system we have described, let us restrict the enhancement of education by technology to the possibility of increasing classroom use of desk and handheld computer (and cell-phone-like) devices. This increase is proceeding at a slow pace today. Will it change to a very rapid build-up?

For the same reasons cited for the major new system earlier described—funding, bureaucracy, nation-state-union politics, and the rest—the Four-Measures rating will be higher than the total of 7 reached for the big systems step, but it will still be too low to become a serious opportunity for a high-technology company to heavily invest in.

Chapter Eleven | A Nuclear Scenario

I ntelligent forecasting, if acted upon with equal intelligence, can sometimes make possible the considerable shaping of the future. Opportunities can be exploited, and disasters can be prevented. Some conceivable future events, even if they appear highly improbable, absolutely demand prior attempts to counter them specifically because if nothing is done, the consequences would be so terrible. Few examples are more suitable for demonstrating this than predicting the possibility of a nuclear bomb attack on the United States and our government's acting to preclude it.

It is beyond being a mere possibility that some nations possessing nuclear bombs will have leaders who are ruthless enemies of the United States. In addition to North Korea and Iran,[1] we can expect several other nations and a number of nonnation terrorist organizations to have the financial means and the relationships that will enable them to acquire nuclear bombs.[2] They can either produce the bombs themselves or obtain them from the

producers of such bombs.[3] It seems foolhardy to not assume that
any group holding generous funds and wanting to possess such
bombs can obtain the engineering information required and
enough enriched uranium or plutonium to assemble at least a
small number of nuclear bombs.[4] The basis for our knowledge of
this possibility stems from reports of the International Atomic
Energy Agency (IAEA), which is the nuclear guardian of the
United Nations, as well as other international and national intelligence agencies. There are numerous other reports of smuggling,
black marketing, the failure to guard the critical materials adequately, evidence of bribery in some areas of the world where fis-
sile materials are stored, and well-documented information about
transfers of the specialized technology.[5]

It has been over 15 years since two distinguished U.S. senators, Dick Lugar and Sam Nunn, began a program in cooperation with Russia to secure the former USSR's enormous stockpile
of nuclear weapons spread over many new nations no longer
under Russia's direct control. Ukraine, Kazakhstan, and other
former USSR states gave up their nuclear weapons, and the
Nunn-Lugar Program is widely judged to have been a success.
The continued Nunn-Lugar effort has led to the removal of
highly enriched uranium from inadequately secured facilities
found in the world.[6] It is to be noted, however, that in 2002, over
100 pounds of nuclear weapons–grade material was removed
from Serbia (why was it there?). Total confident control of every
bit of nuclear weapons materials in the former Soviet Union has
not yet been accomplished.[7]

Dr. Abdul Qadeer Khan, the leader in bomb design for
Pakistan—which, like India, has had nuclear weapons for

years—is known to have traded bomb design know-how with the North Koreans in return for long-range rocket design data.[8]

We should include the following added possibilities:

- **Pakistan.** This nation might be taken over by its extremists. That new leadership might count the United States as an enemy it would not hesitate to damage severely.
- **Iraq.** After the United States' military departs, the three enemy groups, Shiite, Sunni, and Kurd, might go on fighting each other. A few short years from now, one or two or all three might use oil money to buy a modest number of nuclear bombs, perhaps from Pakistan.
- **Afghanistan.** Al-Qaeda and Taliban forces might recapture the country and use opium-derived funds to buy nuclear bombs.

Of course, some will argue that none of the above mentioned entities or North Korea or Iran would ever set off a nuclear bomb in the United States because of the massive retaliation it would expect.[9] But it is a fearsome possibility that these countries or terrorist organizations might secretly station a nuclear bomb in some basement in New York or Los Angeles or Washington. The porosity of the U.S. land and sea borders, together with the fact that it is possible to assemble a bomb in the United States from shielded components that are shipped here clandestinely, suggests the possibility of such plantings. These bombs might well be far inferior to modern U.S. H-bombs as to explosive power. But even one relatively simple, suboptimal nuclear bomb would be capable of killing millions if it were set off in a large American city because the deadly fallout would spread to surrounding areas. "A 10-kiloton bomb detonated at Grand Central Station on a typical work day would likely kill some half a million people and inflict over a trillion dollars in economic damages."[10]

The threat of retaliation by the United States would not be a deterrent.[11] First, it would not be certain which one of the several suspects who could have planted the bomb in the United States actually did it. So against which nation or group would the U.S. leadership perform a massive nuclear response? Also, a strong U.S. retaliatory nuclear attack on Iran, for example, would cause destruction in nations near Iran—Iraq, Syria, Lebanon, Israel, Turkey, Saudi Arabia, Jordan, Egypt, and the Emirates.

Important to be considered also is the possibility of blackmail accompanying the planting of bombs in the United States. Consider, for example, the following scenario: Saddam Hussein, instead of invading Kuwait when he did, waited a few more years until he had available several nuclear bombs. He then placed one in a New York City brownstone together with a radio receiver, some electronics for signal reception and trigger control, and an antenna on the roof. Then, this imagined event goes, he announced to the world that he possessed nuclear bombs and he proved it by setting one off, with the United States' confirming that he indeed had done so. Next, we imagine, he disclosed that he was going to invade Kuwait and take over its oil wells (perhaps claiming Kuwait really belongs to Iraq). He also stated that should the United States attempt to interfere with this plan, he would set off a nuclear bomb that he had already placed in an unnamed U.S. city. The U.S. president, we next suppose, then put forth the counterthreat that should Saddam Hussein do this—invade Kuwait and trigger a nuclear bomb in any American location—the United States would completely destroy Iraq with a massive nuclear response. Saddam replied that he was willing to accept that risk, confident the United States would not launch that counterattack.

What could the U.S. president really have done? He or she might have had to decide not to interfere with Iraq's invasion of Kuwait.

The expected consequences of a nuclear attack on the United States mean that, no matter how low the probability of that attack's occurring, the United States must act to keep it from happening. We are led to the possibility then that the United States must maintain an extremely broad effort to try to discover means to ensure that nuclear attack possibilities cannot become actualities.[12] One theoretical alternative is to create a world totally free of nuclear weapons—hardly a possibility.[13] Another is to remove Saddam Hussein from power before he could develop a nuclear bomb capability. (Did not the United States, perhaps, do exactly that with its invasion of Iraq? But America's leadership did not predict what would happen after eliminating that Iraqi leader. Perhaps not enough possibilities were considered and prepared for.)

RATING THE POSSIBILITY

First, is it probable, (A), that a nuclear bomb might be planted secretly in the United States? If so, (B), when might that happen? Would even the most evil leader of some nation or terrorist group really plan and/or carry out a nuclear attack on a U.S. city?

We should first note that, when it comes to war and terror, things have happened that years before might have been thought too strange, awful, or inhumane to actually happen. A U.S. president in World War II ordered atom bombs to be dropped on the civilian populations of two Japanese cities. An Islamic terrorist group sent suicidal pilots to crash planes into New York and Washington, D.C., buildings, killing thousands and themselves. Individuals and nations have actually committed acts in the past that would have appeared earlier to be of extremely low probability.

Still, intangible, nonnumeric considerations cause us to assign a low 3 to both (A) the probability and (B) the timing. It might happen, we are suggesting, although it is not very likely and it is not likely to be soon. There are several reasons for this optimism. One is that Saddam Hussein, the initiator in this imagined awful possibility, surely would have been concerned with one particular associated possibility. It is that the United States might have anticipated the very act that the Iraqi dictator was planning and might have acted early to counter it.

The effect on the United States, (C), would be profound if the pictured nuclear explosion happened, meaning that 10 is the proper number for (C). Do we claim (although in secrecy as to details) that something really meaningful could be done by the United States to prevent such a happening? Yes. There are overt, covert, technological, economic, and political steps that could be taken early by the United States to lower greatly the chances of success of the kind of nuclear attack we pictured. We give (D) a 7.

In summary:

A. Probability	3
B. Timing	3
C. Impact	10
D. Action potential	7
Total	23

This low total might be a proper evaluation. Yet this is a possibility for which no U.S. president would accept a numeric rating measure alone for the prediction. Instead, any president would insist on mounting a substantial covert counterterrorism program, just in case.

Chapter Twelve | Robotic Birds and No-Casualty Warfare

In this chapter we explore the potential impact of startling technological advances on world affairs with an imaginable example. War casualties have never been received casually by the American people. The war in Iraq, however, has led the country to have much less tolerance for combat deaths and injuries.[1] Yet, to continue to protect national security in the future, U.S. soldiers will inevitably have again to be sent into hostile, highly dangerous territory where the military efforts are not characterized by large-scale traditional warfare involving soldier formations, tanks, and planes but rather by irregular warfare: guerilla activity, urban street and alley combat, road mining, difficult terrain, and ambushes, as exemplified by the military action in Vietnam, Iraq, and Afghanistan. Thus it is likely that America's military leadership will seek aggressively to harness the United States' technological strength and innovative capability so as to develop low-casualty control of world areas where serious threats to U.S. security must be countered.

Are technology advances conceivable to provide for the expected inevitable involvement by U.S. forces while also greatly reducing battle casualties? To answer this question, consider the following fanciful scenario: A U.S. soldier is safely stationed several miles distant from a particular neighborhood in Iraq where he is attempting to locate and eliminate a suspected nest of terrorists and their store of arms. To accomplish this, he has launched a miniaturized mechanical robotic "bird" with which he is in tight communication and is actually "piloting." The soldier-pilot, in other words, is virtually flying himself where the bird is flying. His control of the robot is the equivalent of his being there and holding and aiming it as he would a rifle or a camera.

This robot can fly, see, shoot, send back information, and act in complete response to the soldier-pilot's directions. The soldier-pilot sees on a screen in front of him exactly what the bird's TV camera sees as he orders it to move about in the region under his intended perusal. The robot can hover like a hummingbird, or it can move through the air at a high speed. It can be aimed and focused for specific observing, and it can release its deadly arms at a target when so commanded. The bird is small enough, of course, to go through windows and doorways (and the soldier-pilot may even have dispatched earlier a special other robotic bird "smasher" to create openings as necessary). In appearance the bird is a sort of hybrid of a toy airplane, a handgun, a cell phone with camera, and a handheld computer. It can stay out for hours before it is directed to return to the soldier-pilot's safe base where it can be refueled. These proposed robotic, lightweight, artificial birds would be mass manufactured (in blocks of tens of thousands or more) at a price of a few thousand dollars each.

Is it possible to produce such a mechanism?[2] Might it become a practical development? That this is not impossible is suggested by noting what nature readily offers. An actual living little hummingbird can hover and dart about rapidly. Wild birds like geese and ducks seem easily to display more than the required distance and duration capabilities our postulated robot birds would have to possess.

It would not be easy for a terrorist to escape should he discover that an American robotic bird has tracked him down, is observing him, and is about to kill him. The U.S. soldier-pilot, in his safe and comfortable location, with his high-resolution video, fast and precise controls, and excellent training, is at a dominant advantage in the encounter. That soldier-pilot will have been recruited from a large number of young volunteers who years before had developed high hand-eye coordination skills by many hours of playing complex and speedy computer games and Ping-Pong.[3]

To design and mass-produce these small robots, we would need only to employ the technical specialists available in high-tech defense companies plus those engineers employed in companies making cell phones, cameras, revolvers, and hand-held electronic computers.

Of course, the idea of a robotic bird launched and controlled by a U.S. soldier-pilot in a removed safe location has many variations. One design might be optimized to hunt down al-Qaeda militants and their armament stores in the caves of Afghanistan, and another to seek and eliminate Osama bin Laden himself and his successors and coconspirators. A substantial army of such robots could operate as a coordinated force to sweep through and scour a city, this to locate stores of arms and ammunition and terrorists who might be preparing for their next acts.

It is doubtless far easier to imagine the above described technological development than to actually realize it. But if this possibility were to be brought about, let us observe how broad might be the impact on our influence in the world and national security. Irregular combat with essentially no casualties would revolutionize both warfare and diplomacy. It would provide the oft-cited "police action" capability so badly needed to eliminate rogue action in many areas of the world where terrible horrors are thrust on the civilian populations. Groups of terrorists, unlike nations, could not set up to design and produce their own robots to fight the U.S. robot birds. (We are not speaking here of a war between the United States and China, say, because in such a contest, both sides, we must assume, could produce these flying robots. A "war of the robots" would result and would really be fought and won or lost in the rival factory production lines of China and the United States and between their rival engineering design teams.)

Robotic birds with observation, communication, and action capabilities obviously would also have many extremely interesting applications in the nonmilitary operations of the society. Before citing commercial uses for such flying robots, let us cite a real-life present example that displays some similarities.

America's Global Positioning System (GPS)—signals from satellites in the sky used on Earth to enable the ready determination of precise location—is rare in having provided an opportunity for military technology contractors to participate in a high-growth business in the civilian commercial market. The GPS is critical to the U.S. military for navigation and other purposes, but it has also become basic to an array of commercial products. The signals from the GPS's satellites are key to improved positioning of all things moving on land, at sea, and in the air. This has been highlighted in recent years by the GPS's application to the guiding of automobile drivers. A GPS system could be used to revolutionize commercial airline navigation and traffic control, adding greatly to increased efficiency and safety in all weather conditions as air traffic increases. In addition to government and commercial use of GPS equipment in autos, trucks, airplanes, and ships, individuals increasingly have become purchasers of GPS equipment for their personal use—fishermen, hikers, boaters, surveyors, cell phone users, and others. People deploying hand-held GPS devices to learn where they are and how to get to where they wish to go will surely become a vast market. These applications, already used by over 10 million people, might come to be used by 100 million consumers worldwide.

Here are a few possible future civilian-commercial applications of flying robot birds:[4]

- Robots in place of human inspectors to monitor facilities and animals on ranches, oil fields, and widely spaced chemical facilities
- Nighttime security inspections everywhere
- Low-cost and broad observation of border-crossing areas to prevent illegal immigration
- Automobile and truck traffic control and monitoring, with speeders photographed and warned, traffic light time adjusted

to optimize the flow of vehicles, accidents quickly reached
and observed—all as aids to regular traffic control operations

- 911 callers reached more quickly than ambulances and
police cars, the observations from the flying robots relayed
immediately to provide 911 responders with headstart
information while on their way

Of perhaps greatest importance, it is conceivable that U.S. policy regarding military intervention around the world might be
altered greatly by this high-technology advance. No-casualty
actions accomplished by fleets of robot birds, for example, might
offer the most practical ways to interfere with Iran's plans to possess nuclear bombs, and the United Nations might be cooperative
in approving such actions if Iran continues to ignore its demands.

Is this possibility of robot birds likely to be attained? That is
not easy to know. The development of the propulsion systems for
the desired robots alone, for example, might require years of
invention and perfection. Can we act early on the possibility?
Certainly the exploring of apparatus designs and testing can be
started immediately. We can feel confident in predicting that if
the technological advance can realistically be achieved, it would
create major beneficial changes in warfare and hence in world
social and political situations that are greatly affected by military options and actions.

RATING THE POSSIBILITY

In view of the foregoing discussion, we offer the following ratings
on the possibility that a robotic bird capability will be created by
the United States:

A. Probability	9
B. Timing	8
C. Impact	10
D. Action potential	<u>10</u>
Total	37

In summary, we predict that a large-scale robotic bird capability similar to that described will be created by the U.S. military in less than a decade and that that will allow substantial shaping of future U.S. military activities and foreign policy.

Chapter Thirteen | The Price of Oil

What is today's price for an ounce of gold? Not too many years ago, that figure used to be of primary interest to those in the world making decisions about economic matters. The gold prices are still pertinent to many, as are the prices of copper, wheat, and pork bellies and the wage levels in various industries. Once during presidential election debates a leading candidate lost favor when he was discovered not to know the price of a quart of milk. But one particular price today stands above all others in importance to the widest group of the population, namely, that of a barrel of oil.

The price of gasoline is constantly noted, of course, by automobile users for whom that cost is a serious budget item and by those in the transport business for whom it is also a serious budget item. The cost of crude is a big issue for the managers of industry, and not just the oil industry. It is important to the producers of the huge number of manufactured items that have a petroleum base and of products whose cost of transportation to market is substantial. Most important, the price of oil can be a determining factor in the decision making of the leadership of nations because that price affects economic strength, independence, and stability.

Those who study and must continually redo their forecasted ranges for future oil prices do not fail to give prime attention to one possibility. With lots of expected temporary rises and falls, they predict the price will surely rise with time. This forecast follows from straightforward supply and demand considerations. New oil deposits will be found, but it is considered unlikely they will meet the increase in demand.[1] The developing nations (China, especially, but India and others) will move up in demand per capita, reaching that of the United States and other developed nations. A continuous rise in the price of petroleum, it is thus concluded, will surely follow.[2]

But another possibility merits consideration. It is that the price of oil will settle into a stable range (of perhaps $100 a barrel). This stable price range might be one in which many alternatives to the use of petroleum will become technologically and economically feasible and generally acceptable, and thus the use of alternatives will impact the supply and demand relationship. (Actually, in 1975, President Gerald Ford proposed a plan that, it appears now, would have been achievable and might have altered the supply and demand factor favorably for the United States.)[3]

We start exploring this probability by listing possible future changes in the automobile field, that huge consumer of petroleum. Recall the personal automobile described in Chapter 7, the small electric-petroleum hybrid car that in the decade ahead might provide for a large fraction of personal transportation needs. It would use much less gasoline per mile than present cars.[4] This auto's taking over the traffic lanes for, say, half of the world's city driving would cause a major decrease in petroleum demand.

The other alternative for a future supply to meet the bulk of city driving requirements is the "plug-in" all-electric car, also described in Chapter 7. This possibility amounts to a substitution of electricity for gasoline for powering much of automotive transportation. Naturally, a major shift from autos using petroleum to autos using electricity would require the generation of more electric power and the building of more electric power plants.

Now, the world, including the United States, has plentiful coal supplies, and coal is very productive for energy generation. The problem, however, with substituting coal for petroleum by way of electricity to greatly reduce oil demand for automotive applications is that the process would send too much carbon into the atmosphere.[5] But those who are expert in the applicable engineering processes claim vehemently that it is practical to capture and sequester the carbon products that coal-fired electrical power plants produce.[6] Vattenfall AB, a Swedish power company, as one example, is building a unique coal-fired power plant in East Germany that will inject the carbon dioxide it will emit into caverns existing well below the surface of the earth.

Of course, the application of "clean-coal" ideas to provide ample electric power would add to the price of that power. However, a permanent high, but tolerable, price for a barrel of oil, which we have postulated, will make relatively acceptable that added cost for the removal of the unacceptable gases that coal burning would produce.

Nuclear power offers another means of generating electric power at a price that would fit properly with the automotive industry's shift from pretroleum to electricity. The building of more nuclear power plants and the U.S. public's fear of the nuclear power generation process have been incompatible for decades. Severe dangers have been expected to arise from both the nuclear power plants themselves and from the storage and disposal of the nuclear waste the power plants produce. According to nuclear engineering specialists, however, practical solutions that are technologically and economically sound now can be achieved to address both of these concerns. (See Chapter 14.) The problem appears to be one of communication with the public. It is reasonable to speculate that nuclear-based electric power generation is headed for considerable augmentation in the United States and elsewhere.[7]

What is presented in the foregoing includes the possibility that a future electric battery–operated automobile population—perhaps 100 million cars in America alone—will also become an important way to store electricity. This itself could make a difference of importance in the way solar and wind-generated electricity could become substantial contributors to a successful plan to reduce demand for oil. The capabilities for both solar and wind electric power generation are available today, and the use of these alternatives is expanding. The cost of such systems would come down considerably if they were produced in greater quantities. But that could happen only if a good means of storage were available, since the solar energy cells cannot produce at night and the windmills' propellers cannot turn when the wind is down. Storing the electrical energy in the batteries of the nation's cars and trucks could make it practical to use solar and wind power to make a noticeable contribution to the stability of oil prices.

As mentioned in Chapter 5, biofuel, or agrifuel, is here today but on a very minor scale because ethanol, made from trees, grass, corn, or sugar cane, delivers 30 percent less energy by volume than gasoline. Some scientists believe advances in synthetic biology will lead to much superior new fuels.[8] Today, autos and trucks are available that can burn a mixture of gasoline and ethanol, and that combination fuel is already procurable in a small fraction of filling stations. Many believe that ethanol from corn is the answer to greatly reducing the demand for petroleum. But ethanol production requires so much land and water (to create only a bit more energy than is needed to produce it) that it is unrealistic to expect it to reduce oil demand substantially. It is nowhere near as likely a possibility as ethanol produced from sugar cane and from trees, and, fortunately, there are other friendly countries where those resources are generously available. Scientists at the California Institute of Technology are working to produce butanol—far superior to ethanol as a fuel—from tree or treelike matter (not food materials) by using new microbes specially designed and created for the task.[9] At the presumed high but tolerable steady oil price, it is thus reasonable to consider ethanol and butanol meaningful contributors in the future. They might well take their places with the other alternatives to petroleum that together might hold back the latter's otherwise steady price rise.[10]

Improvements certainly can be made in city mass transit to reduce the need for personal auto use, and this is a likely future development with oil prices remaining high. Much auto fuel is used up because of traffic density in cities and because of such annoyingly frequent negatives as the need for extra travel to locate a parking place. The shift to smaller cars would increase spaces in parking lots.

Companies seeking locations for expanded facilities might be led in the future to locate them some 20 or so miles from present cities where land for homes, schools, shopping, and so on might be developed very near the new work areas, this making walking or short rides common. The nearby larger city would be conveniently reachable to round out employees' living requirements while their overall need for petroleum would be reduced.

China is particularly often cited as destined to inflate demand for oil enormously as it continues to expand industrially. Simultaneously, it turns out, Russia's enormous Siberian region is equally often described as the world's largest unexplored land mass and a likely impressive source of oil. It is often speculated that China and Russia may one day come to war with each other because the sparse Russian population in this huge area shares a long boundary with China whose enormous population invites boundary crossings. Perhaps, however, a more likely possibility than war is a cooperative Russia-China development of new oil output from Siberia to its neighbor, China. The result might be a meeting of China's oil needs with less adverse contribution to the supply and demand equation that sets the world price of oil.

The expected shortage of petroleum supply in the future, the possibly steady high price for available petroleum, and the concern in the United States over the dependency on imported petroleum have given rise to the proposition of many substitutes for that energy-rich substance extracted from the Earth. The quest, however, seems too often focused on single substitutes (such as ethanol, windmills, or nuclear power). We are suggesting here that a steady high oil price combined with the development of a wide array of alternatives[11]—no one of which alone can replace petroleum—may turn out to be the most realistic possibility.[12]

RATING THE POSSIBILITY

We recognize the limitations of a rating that assigns numbers to key aspects of the world's petroleum supply and demand issue. It is a complicated problem overall with numerous political and other unmeasurable dimensions. We nevertheless offer the following rating for the possibility that the price of oil will remain in the $100 range in the long term:

A. Probability	7
B. Timing	9
C. Impact	9
D. Action potential	9
Total	34

This possibility appears to deserve serious eligibility as a solid prediction by predictors in many aspects of the world's operations, both private and governmental.

Chapter Fourteen | The SuperGrid Electric Power System

In 2005 Chauncey Starr, formerly the president of the Electric Power Research Institute (the electric power industry's collaborative R&D organization), proposed an electric power grid that could provide a reliable and plentiful national supply of electricity generated by methods that do not contribute to global warming.[1] This SuperGrid concept is based on a network of air-cooled nuclear power plants (today's nuclear installations are water cooled) with all the equipment located underground for both safety and security. The nuclear waste material would also be kept underground for long-term storage.

New nuclear power technology makes possible a "fail-safe" design—a cooling failure no longer leading to a runaway meltdown "through the Earth to China"—that is less costly and takes less time to build. Moreover, the proposed individual generators would not be of enormous size and capacity, with the substantial number of generators to be built giving rise to manufacturing cost reduction because of the large-scale production.[2] Even prominent environmentalists grudgingly recognize that nuclear power is "green," unlike the carbon-product-spewing coal that currently fuels most of the nation's electricity generation.

Christine Todd Whitman, former Environmental Protection Agency chief, writing in *BusinessWeek* (September 17, 2007, page 102), said, "We have a choice to make: We can either continue the 30-year debate about whether we should embrace nuclear energy, or we can accept its practical advantages. Expanding nuclear energy makes both environmental and business sense." So the installation of nuclear reactors is no longer being totally ruled out by those with the decision powers, only some of whom remain skeptical.[3] The highly negative environmental changes now in evidence have convinced many that carbon emissions might be a greater danger to the world than nuclear accidents or radioactive waste.[4]

The SuperGrid's power plants, it is proposed, would be spaced miles apart and would utilize a countrywide tunnel system of superconducting cables. Unlike today's electricity transmission network, which simply evolved randomly as the nation's needs expanded, these cables would allow large quantities of electrical energy to move efficiently over the entire United States as needed. Air cooling would eliminate the need for locating nuclear generators near rivers or oceans.

Superconductivity refers to a property of certain materials that can conduct electricity without resistance losses—the major shortcoming of conventional electric cables—when these special materials are chilled to extremely low temperatures. Some of the electricity generated would be used to electrolyze water into its hydrogen and oxygen constituents and then to compress the hydrogen into liquid form to chill the cables. (At the points along the grid where the superconducting cables would offload electric power into local distribution systems, hydrogen could be made available, thus serving as the foundation for a hydrogen infrastructure that is now lacking.)[5]

Two or three decades of time and the expending of hundreds of billions of dollars would be required to complete the SuperGrid if it were planned ultimately to take over entirely from the existing patchwork electric power system. By then, if the United States' current annual growth rate in electricity demand continues as expected, the nation's electricity needs surely will have more than doubled.

The SuperGrid would push the limits of our engineering experience but not of our science. The brand-new transcontinental power grid would be a daunting construction project, but accomplishing it is certainly a possibility from the purely scientific and engineering standpoint. Will it be too expensive? The following abstract from the decades-old personal notes given us by a member of President Nixon's cabinet is interestingly pertinent:[6]

In 1970 the Cabinet listened as Dr. Glen Seaborg, then head of the Atomic Energy Commission, recited findings from his study of U.S. energy needs. Seaborg's intended message was clear—our country was losing its energy independence as we depleted our oil reserves at twice the rate we were replacing them.

Seaborg forecasted that in a few short years, America would find itself at the mercy of Middle East oil sheiks, who could then cripple us economically and humble us politically. He concluded by proposing a program designed to make our country 90 percent energy self-sufficient in five years.

As Seaborg finished, I looked around the Cabinet Room. There we sat, a rather standard group of American policy makers—one-time lawyers, economists, business executives, and history professors. Not one, including me, had ever been exposed to five minutes of advanced scientific education. Though we could all appreciate Seaborg's concern, not one of us was capable of following fully his science-based rationale. Our dimness of comprehension found us inclined to dismiss what we had heard as just a technical specialist's opinion.

Eventually economist Arthur Burns, the Federal Reserve chairman, spoke up with an economist's question:

"How much would all this cost?" Arthur asked Seaborg.

"Three billion dollars a year over five years," Seaborg replied.

Well!! Maybe we couldn't grasp Seaborg's analysis, but we sure could understand $15 billion! That was real money, even in Washington. As an administration that had come to Washington promising fiscal responsibility, to spend $15 billion for something that strained our comprehension seemed the height of folly. The president thanked Dr. Seaborg for a "cogent" presentation, and the Cabinet meekly went on to other business.

We all now know what happened. Within three years the entire world was to suffer the consequences of our noncomprehension. In late 1973 the Middle East oil sheiks, displeased with America's Israel policy, shut off flow of their liquid gold. Before the end of the decade they would slam a cowering and vulnerable world with an eightfold hike in oil prices. Failure to invest a paltry $15 billion ended up costing an oil-hungry world hundreds of billions of dollars.

The SuperGrid electrical system might be categorized as one of high initial cost, but after about the first decade of operation, the potential annual savings could exceed the initial expenditures. Making practical the plug-in autos described in Chapter 7 and thus eliminating the U.S. dependence on petroleum imports, plus holding down petroleum prices, might alone justify the network's installation cost. Beyond that, diminishing war potentials, strengthening international economic stability, and curbing global warming would all yield huge benefits. (Consider the half-trillion-dollar costs of the Iraq War and other possible future conflicts that could arise out of contests for access to limited petroleum supply—aside from the wars' casualty tragedies that are beyond monetary assessments.)

The possibility exists that the United States' creation of a nuclear SuperGrid might well cause Europe, China, India, and others to build similar grids later. The United States' technological expertise and prowess in nuclear power due to our past nuclear power employment in our aircraft carriers and submarines, together with the pioneering of this SuperGrid, would almost ensure large U.S. nuclear equipment exports. This would have positive repercussions on the economy of the United States as it heads for a population of 400 million.

RATING THE POSSIBILITY

There are not many possible major technology advances whose arrivals could offer as many benefits to the United States as might the SuperGrid. When we list possibilities for the long-range future, we should not hesitate to include those that ought to be pursued simply because they should. Sometimes, the society, even if it is slow, does do what is right.[7]

In choosing (A), the probability it will be brought into existence, however, we must be realistic. It would be the nation's greatest project,[8] and the prejudice against nuclear power in America is still high.[9] No matter how unjustified this public feeling may be when alternatives are competently assessed, it exists and it will stand in the way. For (A), accordingly, we rate the probability at 6. The very boldness of the plan, the size of the investment, and the fact that doing it means committing to a huge scale of endeavor, all taken together, means that it is not sensible to imagine its happening soon. Accordingly, we allot (B) a 3. Creating an electric power infrastructure of this breadth obviously would greatly affect industry expansion, national economic and technological strength, and national security. Thus, (C) rates a 10. Action ahead of time would be possible and effective, leading to a figure of 10 for (D).

In summary:

A. Probability	6
B. Timing	3
C. Impact	10
D. Action potential	10
Total	29

This is an above-average rating for a possibility. It deserves strong consideration as a prediction. The electric power industry

should consider acting ahead and early to ensure participation if this possibility begins to take root and becomes a
reality. If it indeed happens, as it seems perhaps it should,
some technological companies might find it will constitute
for them the greatest opportunity in their history.

Chapter Fifteen | The Medical Practice Internet Channel

A physician at some future time, let us imagine, is seeing a patient who has arrived in his office with severe bronchitis. The doctor turns to the keyboard of his computer, touches two or three buttons, and then enters "bronchitis." The number 14,263 appears on his screen indicating the system has that many physicians' reports regarding recent treatment of bronchitis. To this number he pays little attention as he further enters: "male, age 82, heart pacemaker, hospitalized with pneumonia last year, one and a half degree temperature, somewhat higher than average blood pressure," etc., etc. about this patient, each entry reducing the computer's displayed number, which soon decreases from the original of over 10,000 to only 17.

The doctor now proceeds to read each of the 17 one-page reports of patients' symptoms and complaints, tests performed, treatments the other physicians chose, and the results attained with their patients.

He finds that the precise treatment he is considering has been generally applied but that a minority of doctors reported somewhat different approaches. He ponders this information as he makes his decision on how to handle his patient now. He has been provided, we note, with much of what he might have received had he spoken directly with the 17 other specialists having very similar cases. After he has finished with his patient, he will enter into the system his pertinent data, including his treatment and its results. (He could not have accessed these 17 reports without the Web system designed for that purpose even if he were willing to spend a year.)

A small bit of this aid is available today to a practicing physician, really no more than access to a library file of published articles—nothing resembling the equivalent of multiple opinions by fellow specialists on their choices and results of treatments for patients in similar situations.[1] Yet the art and technology available today make this imagined Internet system readily designable and economically sound.

Of course, the detailed design of the basic architecture and programming of the system will require a major effort by a team consisting of both computer systems engineers and practicing physicians. The costs for this design and start-up effort would be very substantial, but the possible benefits offered by the system to the practice of medicine might well greatly exceed the initial and the operating costs. The physicians would pay a monthly fee for the privilege of entering the Internet channel plus a fee for each inquiry. They would receive credits to their accounts for all of the reports of results they enter into the network. The system might also countenance an appropriate amount of advertising alongside the information displays.

The creation of this future Medical Practice Internet Channel need not wait for a government decision to develop it and allocate the required funds. There is the possibility that it might happen as a risk investment by some private enterprise seeking profits. Perhaps a group of leading medical schools might collaborate to be the originators. With the income likely to exceed the expenses, funding would be generated to steadily improve and expand the system.

This possibility might belong in the category of those with a high probability of occurrence because they so clearly should be created. That is because the imagined system is so economically and societally advantageous. With this system physicians will be able to practice medicine on a significantly higher quality level. New medical specialties and new professions will arise to make possible this new extension of the physicians' professional powers. Diagnoses and treatments will improve, and the understanding of what causes diseases and what cures them will reach a higher plateau.

This electronic information system does not replace the physician; rather, it assists the physician. The partnership of medical profession and network has the potential of encompassing much more of the information useful in the practice of medicine. It makes possible utilization of the experiences of many doctors with many patients to provide the best treatment for any one patient.

The system would offer more than the pooling of information. It would be designed to notice whether or not a particular assembly of symptoms and treatment has been presented to it before. If the usual tests are being called for, for example, then the system would make no comment. If, however, the proposed tests by the physician appear to be unnecessary, irrelevant, or incomplete, then the system would suggest the more commonly ordered ones. The system would not simply take in information and turn it back out when tapped. It would be capable of comparing the incoming with the stored information.

The system's rules of comparison will be subject to continual updating, resulting from experience with the system or stemming from improvements in medical practice. Indeed, enhancement of medical care will be accelerated by the availability of the system as well as by the efforts of new "systems-physician" specialists—those whose efforts are focused on analyzing and improving the system's operation.

Practicing physicians will at times reject certain of the computer's responses as useless, self-evident, or unimportant, and the system will be programmed to take note of such criticisms by practicing doctors. Over a period of time, it will avoid sending responses that provoke physician rejects if enough of them accumulate. If the system tells the physician that the proposed tests are "incomplete" and the physician chooses the "disagree" option, the system will learn that the physician views fewer tests as satisfactory. The system responses will change to reflect the physicians' majority responses. Also, if more and more doctors call for more facts than they see on their screens, the system will automatically note this and will begin requesting additional facts when physicians report in. By extending the physicians' thought processes and by their learning to employ fully the information available to them, the system will improve the practice of medicine.

RATING THE POSSIBILITY

Imagine that a group of the nation's top-ranked medical schools believe strongly that they should join in an effort to create this Medical Practice Internet Channel. They feel confident that it should happen and that they can cause it to happen, a self-fulfilled prophecy. They contemplate jointly funding a small first step—that is, the preparation of a proposal that they might present to a select number of philanthropic foundations that regularly provide funds for research to those medical schools.

The proposal will describe a start-up plan to create the Internet channel including in detail such issues as proposed arrangements with existing computer software companies to design and operate the channel in close cooperation with a medical advisory board furnished by the medical schools; a financial plan for the start-up and early years of operation before the volume of operations reaches the level for self-sustainability; eventual profit-sharing potentials; the architectural design of the system for access, inquiries, screening, storing, and response to physician inquiries; initial creation of an adequate information inventory of symptoms and treatments so that the channel can be of valuable aid to the early physician users; and a set of safeguards in its use to minimize exposure to frivolous class-action lawsuits.

The preparation of this proposal itself will require considerable effort and time. The medical school group may seek and expect to raise funds for this step alone.

This possibility may deserve being given the status of a prediction meriting early action to become a self-fulfilled prophecy.

It is certainly doable. The return on invested capital should be acceptable. It can be designed and made operable in a reasonably short time. It need not require government approval and regulation.[2] Although this sequence of events seems likely to us, what numbers do we recommend for the four usual measures? They are the following:

A. Probability	9
B. Timing	9
C. Impact	10
D. Action potential	10
Total	38

The total figure is high enough for the possibility to be made a prediction.

What will the American Medical Association, the *New England Journal of Medicine*, the U.S. Department of Health and Human Services, and the U.S. Surgeon General have to say? We do not know. We see no reason, however, to hold back on the prediction that the Internet will include a Medical Practice Internet Channel in the not too distant future.

Chapter Sixteen | The Next War

Because of the United States' experience in Iraq, most Americans may now assume it to be extremely unlikely that this country will become involved in the near future in a major military action and occupation anywhere else in the world. The United States might find itself with a need to dispatch warships to some region. But would Congress approve the commitment of a large force to engage in what would appear to be a multiyear conflict, one likely to result in high casualties and to require expenditures of hundreds of billions of dollars? Is that now not a realistic possibility? Perhaps. But consider the following scenario:

We recall that the 9/11 disaster was planned and executed by a terrorist team consisting almost entirely of Saudi Arabians. Osama bin Laden, the leader of al-Qaeda, is a Saudi. In fact, he is from a leading family in the Saudi society's upper echelon. Also, every so often we note a report that a few young Saudis have attempted some sort of action against the Saudi government and that the effort has failed. But suppose that one day a few years from now, we are startled to learn that assassinations of some

Saudi government leaders have just occurred and that there have been takeovers of some of the oil fields in Saudi Arabia.[1] Imagine also that it then quickly becomes clear that a full-blown revolution has begun in that country, this because the Saudi ruling family asks for immediate U.S. military aid.

The U.S. president, we go on to suppose, responds quickly. American planes begin landing troops and armament, and U.S. bases are established promptly in Saudi Arabia. Attempts to defend, regain, and control petroleum facilities and the surrounding areas are begun in earnest by the U.S. military.

A clear lack of anticipation and preparation for this situation will be apparent. We will experience a sudden realization of the inadequacy of intelligence that should have enabled the expectancy of, and the planning and readiness for, this surprising development. It is especially shocking to discover that the takeover forces in Saudi Arabia are numerous and strongly equipped.

We go on imagining. Suppose that the U.S. involvement turns out to be not at all controversial. The issue, that is, is not like the United States' entry into Iraq. All agree that Saudi Arabia, having the richest petroleum deposits in the world, cannot be allowed to be a war zone with the oil supply cut off. Thus, European countries plus Japan, Australia, and Canada all immediately send troops, and an American general is assigned to be the commander of the large international force that begins to be organized furiously to take back all seized oil fields and to protect the rest.

Soon it is discovered that because of the traditional Arab-Persian, Sunni-Shiite enmity, Iran is found to have been active in supplying the revolutionary forces. (Iran likes seeing the Saudi oil production slowed and oil prices exploding.) Also, the workers in the Saudi oil facilities seem to be more on the side of the revolutionaries than on the side of the Saudi government.

The United States finds itself involved in what looks to be a new major war effort. What should we imagine will happen next?

It is a reasonable possibility that the international armies will begin to succeed in taking back the major oil production facilities and setting up strongly to guard them. They will also gain control of airports, city centers, and large industrial installations in Saudi Arabia. But that will not mean that the fighting has ended or that the United States and allied forces have experienced victory and can go home. Consistent with what we have described is that warfare will continue with every important sector of Saudi Arabia under undiminished sabotage attack—particularly, of course, all oil-related facilities. The oil flow rate from Saudi Arabia thus will be greatly reduced, and the world price per barrel will reach a frighteningly high level. Were the international force to leave or reduce its efforts significantly, it is clear that Saudi Arabia petroleum operations might be brought to a standstill by the continued revolutionary effort.

As the frantic days change to months, the United States and the other nations providing the controlling forces might well add up the casualties and the costs of the warfare, together with their lack of confidence in the vital petroleum production, and they will all agree this situation cannot continue. They will start looking for ways to get out but also to find a way to secure oil production if they do leave. They will at first find this to be a problem with no

solution. But then the possibilities might come to be seen as
including something quite different from the situation in Iraq.

Saudi Arabia does not have three groups (Shiite, Sunni, and
Kurd) intent on killing each other. Consequently, peace and stability will seem to be realizable, but only if the Saudi leadership,
hardly a popularly elected government, were to vacate or be
deposed. Let us also imagine that it is discovered that Osama bin
Laden is long gone and that the present, real leaders of this Saudi
Arabia revolution—and the revolution is seen as what it surely
is—are young educated Saudis, some with degrees from
American and British universities.[2]

Strange and totally unacceptable as it might first appear to
be, the revolutionary leaders on the one hand and the United
States with its international partners on the other will start to
focus upon the idea of actually allowing the revolutionaries to
take over from the elderly royal family dictatorship. These events
would play out only, of course, if negotiations seemed able to conclude with a stable Saudi Arabia, one operating with friendly
understandings with the United States and its allies, the oil then
flowing smoothly and the Saudi economy flourishing safely under
the control of new, responsible, younger Saudis, dollars flowing
in as bountifully as the oil flows out, all foreign military forces
gone, and no more warfare and casualties.

Envisioning the benefits, when compared with long and continued casualties and no oil flow, could become a compelling basis
for a deal. Meanwhile, before such a war settlement conceivably
could take place, the oil price rise would harshly affect the world.
A recession might set in everywhere, harming severely the world's
economy and the governments' incomes and expenditures and

trade balances, including those of the United States. These damaging developments would be the impetus for implementing the solution.

That the Saudi "oil well revolution" could result in this odd ending is extremely peculiar, of course, but is it not a possibility? Recall that Colonel Quadaffi of Libya—whom the United States once categorized as one of the top evil leaders of the world, along with the leaders of North Korea and Iran—amazingly and suddenly decided that instead of seeking to possess nuclear bombs and engaging in destroying Western passenger planes, he could choose to behave, get financial help to develop his oil industry, and enjoy peace and high income.

The occurrence of this Saudi revolution and its conclusion might be deemed to be of very low probability. Should it nevertheless actually happen, however, it would be seen later as inexcusable that it was not anticipated.

RATING THE POSSIBILITY

The foregoing contains extremely imaginary content; it requires a severe stretch to assign numerical ratings and deem them to be definitive enough for prediction decisions. Yet it is difficult to put aside this possibility once it is conceived. Is this Saudi oil war at all really likely? We deem it worth a 5 for (A). It could happen sooner or later; the timing is certainly a guess. We choose 5 for (B). Would it have a big effect on the world if it does occur as described? Definitely yes; (C) is clearly a 10. Might we be able to act so as to improve the future if we predict this revolution will happen and then it does indeed occur? Yes, for sure. (D) is a 10.

In summary:

A. Probability	5
B. Timing	5
C. Impact	10
D. Action potential	<u>10</u>
Total	30

With this total, it would seem to be intelligent forecasting to predict that this possibility will become an actuality, rather than to ignore it. If this turns out wrong, relatively little will be lost. If right, the gain in shaping the future could be great.

|Postlude

Predicting the future with high accuracy is virtually impossible. But strategic forecasting is mandatory for sound business management. Waiting—planning to react after the future unfolds—is insufficient. Instead, business leaders should act ahead of time so as to shape the future, maximizing the potentially positive developments and minimizing the negative ones.

Management should create a voluminous list of future possibilities, some of which will be turned into predictions. The listed possibilities should be rated by the Four-Measures approach, and management priority should be allocated to those possibilities scoring highest. The Four-Measures quantitative scoring should be a guide, with parallel qualitative study of the possibilities essential for the selecting of those that will become predictions.

Wide coverage should characterize the possibilities list. To ensure this, analytical and imaginative extrapolations should be made from the past and present. Missing links holding up developments should be identified as should pertinent science and technology advances. Apparent Sure Things regarding future happenings should be challenged. Possible government actions and business pattern changes should be noted. Sudden discontinuities in all phenomena affecting world business should be anticipated and probed.

The value of strategic forecasting will be set not only by the degree of a business management's understanding of its specific area but also by the occurrences in the outside world. The forecasting effort hence must include surveying—however unrealistically or incompletely—such Big Externalities.

Some of the predictions basic to shaping the future will turn out wrong. Hence both the possibilities list and the forecast must be updated continually.

|Notes

INTRODUCTION

1. In comparison with other animals, the human species appears to be unique in its prediction activities. See Daniel T. Gilbert and Timothy D. Wilson, "Prospection: Experiencing the Future," *Science*, vol. 317, September 7, 2007, p. 1357.

2. James Surowiecki, *The Wisdom of Crowds*, Knopf, New York, 2005. See also *New York Academy of Science Magazine*, Spring 2008, p. 15.

3. See Daniel Sarewitz, Roger A. Pielke, and Radford Byerly, editors, *Prediction: Science, Decision Making, and the Future of Nature*, Island Press, Washington, D.C., 2000, pp. 42 and 196.

4. See, for instance, Ben Bernanke, "Irreversibility, Uncertainty, and Cyclical Investment," *Quarterly Journal of Economics*, February 1983.

5. See Francis X. Diebold, *Elements of Forecasting*, 4th ed., South-Western, Florence, Ky., 2006.

6. There are even forecasters of what forecasters will forecast. See "Weather Patterns," *Economist*, April 21, 2007, p. 86.

7. See "Science and Technology," *Economist* (London), August 18, 2007, vol. 384, p. 69.

203

8. See William A. Sherden, *The Fortune Sellers*, Wiley, New York, 1998.

9. See Andreas S. Weigend with Neil A. Gershenfeld, editor, *Time Series Prediction*, Addison-Wesley, Reading, Mass., 1994, p. 529.

10. See Joshua J. Yates, "Managing the Future," *Hedgehog Review*, vol. 10, no. 1, Spring 2008, p. 52.

11. Nassim Nicholas Taleb, *The Black Swan*, Random House, New York, 2007, p. 203.

12. For a sophisticated, deep discussion of what constitutes scientific thinking, see Peter Dear, *The Intelligibility of Nature: How Science Makes Sense of the World*, University of Chicago Press, Chicago, 2006.

13. See Robert W. Bly, *The Science in Science Fiction*, BenBella Books, Dallas, Tex., 2005. See also Michio Kaku, *Physics of the Impossible*, Doubleday, New York, 2008.

14. Even the great early economist Adam Smith, the author of the classic *The Wealth of Nations*, seemed blind to the start of the Industrial Revolution that was changing English life even as he was writing. See David Warsh, *Knowledge and the Wealth of Nations*, W.W. Norton, New York, 2007, p. 48.

CHAPTER ONE

1. That the largest companies do not originate all technology advance is no recent development. The key ideas in the following fields were conceived by individuals not employed by large companies: atomic energy, computers, cellophane, color photography, the cyclotron, DDT, FM radio, foam rubber, inertial guidance, insulin, lasers, the Polaroid camera, radar, rockets, streptomycin, penicillin, the Model T Ford, the telephone, light bulbs, the phonograph, vacuum tubes, xerography, and the zipper.

2. See *Economist*, October 25, 2008, p. 13, regarding the sudden collapse of IBM's mainframe business.

3. See John Orton, *The Story of Semiconductors*, Oxford University Press, New York, 2004.

4. But then IBM did not see that hardware and software could both prosper best as separate businesses, thus offering an opening for Microsoft.

5. See Simon Ramo, *The Business of Science*, by Farrar, Straus & Giroux, New York, 1988, ch. 3.

6. See Christine Pulliam, "Space Telescope," *Inside Smithsonian Research*, Autumn 2007, p. 8.

7. TRW merged with Northrop Grumman in December 2002.

8. See also Michael D. Griffin, administrator, "The Space Economy," NASA 50th Anniversary Lecture Series, National Aeronautics and Space Administration (NASA), September 17, 2007.

9. See Michael Korda, *Ike: An American Hero*, HarperCollins, New York, 2007, p. 203.

10. See, for instance, Conrad Black, *Franklin Delano Roosevelt*, Perseus Books Group, New York, 2003.

11. See Allen W. Dulles, "The Present Situation in Germany," *Foreign Affairs*, vol. 82, no. 6, December 13, 1945, p. 3.

12. See "Leaders: From Helicopter to Hawk," *Economist*, July 21, 2007, p. 13.

13. See, for example "Legislative Forecast for 2008," posted by Congressman Ron Paul, March 27, 2008.

14. See, for example, Thomas L. Friedman, "Bailout (and Buildup)," *New York Times*, October 22, 2008, p. A29. Also James Grant, "After the Crash," *Foreign Affairs*, November/December 2008, p. 141; Arthur B. Laffer, "The Age of Prosperity Is Over," *New York Times*, October 27, 2008, p. A19; and Laffer, "Finance and Economics: But Will It Work," *Economist*, October 18, 2008, p. 83.

CHAPTER TWO

1. The Sarbanes-Oxley Act of 2002, commonly called SOX, is a U.S. federal law that was passed in response to major corporate and accounting scandals (Enron, Tyco, and so on) which had resulted in a decline of public trust in earnings and assets reporting. This legislation established enhanced reporting standards and detailed disclosure rules, and it mandated criminal penalties for violations on corporate board members and managers and on public accounting firms.

CHAPTER THREE

1. As a convincing illustration of the employment of gifted imagination coupled with competent analysis to create scenarios of future possible developments, see what deserves to be labeled a classic text by Peter Schwartz, *The Art of the Long View*, Currency Paperback, Doubleday, New York, 1966.
2. Space Technology Laboratories was originally a separate corporation founded and wholly owned by TRW. It became the Space Technology Sector of Northrop Grumman when TRW was acquired by Northrop Grumman in December 2002.
3. The EADS plane had been built, flown, and tested. In contrast, the plane Boeing seemed likely to offer would be newly created from parts of various older models, had not yet been built, and had less fuel-carrying capacity than the EADS plane.
4. The Buy America Act created "public interest" exceptions.
5. Boeing itself serves as a case study in how globalization can cut both ways. By its own statements, the $66 billion company could never stay competitive if it were not for the benefits of global alliances. Today a substantial portion of the components of all Boeing commercial

models are supplied by foreign contractors, and that fraction rises to more than 40 percent on its new 787 Dreamliner.

6. With the American dollar falling dramatically in relation to the euro, assembling the tanker in America would lower the manufacturing costs.

7. Such a dismal prospect is not unprecedented. Consider the Department of Energy's multidecade attempt to create a safe storage repository for spent nuclear waste at Yucca Mountain, Nevada.

CHAPTER FOUR

1. Small signals can sometimes yield a decisive advantage to those who detect them. See Mark Penn, *Microtrends: The Small Forces Behind Tomorrow's Big Changes*, Twelve/Hachette Book Group, New York, 2007.

2. Formerly vice chair of the Federal Reserve System Board of Governors and director of the White House Office of Management and Budget (OMB); quoted in Daniel Sarewitz, Roger A. Pielke, and Radford Byerly, editors, *Prediction: Science, Decision Making, and the Future of Nature*, Island Press, Washington, D.C., 2000, p. 303.

3. James Hodgson, once a Lockheed Corporation vice president, then U.S. secretary of labor, then ambassador to Japan.

4. From Peggy Anne Salz, "Intelligent Use of Information Is a Powerful Corporate Tool," *Wall Street Journal*, April 27, 2006, p. A10.

CHAPTER FIVE

1. See Peter W. Huber and Mark P. Mills, *The Bottomless Well*, Basic Books, New York, 2005.

2. While waxing optimistically, let us also say that the nuclear reaction alters the liquid coal's chemistry, making its future burning

less polluting, and further, let us imagine that we wait a few years before extracting the liquid so that any radioactivity engendered will have died down.

3. See Daniel Nocera, MIT chemist, *Science*, vol. 35, February 9, 2007, p. 789. See also *Science*, vol. 321, August 1, 2008, p. 620.

4. See "Science and Technology: Storing Electricity," *Economist*, August 18, 2007, p. 70.

5. John Mathews of Macquarie University. See *Scientific American*, June 2007, p. 20. Also see Patrick Barta, "Jatropha Plant Gains Steam," *Wall Street Journal*, August 24, 2007, p. A1.

6. See Donald Kennedy, "Climate: Game Over" *Science*, vol. 317, July 27, 2007, p. 425.

7. See "Business: The Flavour of Cool Cultural Filtering," *Economist*, July 28, 2007, p. 73.

8. See Lamar Alexander, "Nurturing the Next Einsteins," editorial, *Science*, vol. 307, February 18, 2005, p. 1013.

9. William A. Wulf, then president of the National Academy of Engineering, editorial in *Science*, vol. 316, June 2007, p. 1253.

10. See Walter Isaacson, *Einstein*, Simon & Schuster, New York, 2007, p. ix.

11. *Predictable Surprises* by Max Bazerman and Michael Watkins (Harvard Business School Press, Boston, 2004)—a book that deserves to be rated a classic for its pertinence, clarity, and credibility— describes a number of important occurrences that came as surprises but should have been predicted.

CHAPTER SIX

1. See Vivek Ranadivé, *The Power to Predict*, McGraw-Hill, New York, 2006, pp. 42–44.

2. Nassim Nicholas Taleb, author of *The Black Swan*, Random House, New York, 2007, p. 136.

3. See Theodore Modis, *Predictions*, Simon & Schuster, New York, 1992, pp. 61–62.

CHAPTER SEVEN

1. See David Kiley, "The Little Engines That Would," *BusinessWeek*, April 7, 2008, pp. 90–91.

2. See R. James Woolsey, "Gentlemen, Start Your Plug-Ins," *Wall Street Journal*, December 30, 2006. Also see *Wall Street Journal*, March 26, 2007, p. A12.

CHAPTER EIGHT

1. See Daniel Jackson, Martyn Thomas, and Lynette I. Millett, editors, *Software for Dependable Systems: Sufficient Evidence?* Computer Science and Telecommunications Board (CSTB), National Research Council (NRC), National Academies Press, Washington, D.C., 2007.

2. See Frank Barnaby, *How to Build a Nuclear Bomb*, Granta Publications, London, 2003.

3. See Roddam Narasimha, Arvind Kumar, Stephen P. Cohen, and Rita Guenther, editors, *Science and Technology to Counter Terrorism: Proceedings of an Indo-U.S. Workshop*, Committee on International Security and Arms Control, National Academy of Sciences, National Academies Press, Washington, D.C., 2007.

CHAPTER NINE

1. See C. Fred Bergsten, Bates Gill, Nicholas R. Lardy, and Derek Mitchell, *China: The Balance Sheet*, Public Affairs/Perseus Books, New York, 2006.

2. See *Foreign Affairs*, vol. 86, no. 6, pp. 94–97.

3. See Council on Foreign Relations, *U.S.-China Relations*, Independent Task Force Report No. 59, New York and Washington, D.C., April 2007.

4. See Loretta Chao, "China Mobile Push Pinches Rivals," *Wall Street Journal*, August 23, 2007, p. B4.

5. See Robert W. Fogel, "Capitalism & Democracy in 2040," *Daedalus*, Summer 2007, p. 87.

6. Unfortunately, China may become the earth's foremost polluter and destroyer of the environment. China and India are now often predicted to become the two largest economic powers of the world, but their worsening environments may limit both. See Elizabeth C. Economy, "The Great Leap Backward?" *Foreign Affairs*, September/October 2007, p. 39. Also see Joshua Hammer, "A Prayer for the Ganges," *Smithsonian*, November 2007, p. 75.

7. Some in the United States rate China's rapidly increasing trade surplus as due to China's improper manipulation of its currency exchange ratios and its beyond-legal export subsidies.

8. See Aliya Sternstein, "Lawmaker Predicts U.S.-China Space Race,"*Congress Daily*, January 11, 2008. See also Pavel Podvig and Hui Zhang, "Russian and Chinese Responses to U.S. Military Plans in Space," American Academy of Arts and Sciences Occasional Paper, Cambridge, Mass., 2008.

9. See http://en.wikipedia.org/wiki//U.S._National_Space_Policy.

10. See Donald A. Beattie, *ISScapades: The Crippling of America's Space Program*, Collector's Guide Publishing/Apogee Books, Burlington, Ontario, 2007.

11. See Choe-Jin Lee, *A Troubled Peace: U.S. Policy and the Two Koreas*, Johns Hopkins University Press, Baltimore, Md., 2006.

12. China, unlike the United States, seems to have friendly relations with Iran and so might be helpful there. See John W. Garver, *China*

and *Iran in a Post-Imperial World*, University of Washington Press, Seattle, Wash., 2006.

13. In May 2007, it was announced that China is investing billions of dollars in the large U.S. private equity firm The Blackstone Group.

CHAPTER ELEVEN

1. For evidence that interest on the part of Iran in nuclear bomb technology began in the 1970s, see Colin Dueck and Ray Takeyh, "Iran's Nuclear Challenge," *Political Science Quarterly*, vol. 122, November 2, 2007, p. 189.

2. See William C. Potter, Charles D. Ferguson, and Leonard D. Spector, "The Four Faces of Nuclear Terror and the Need for a Prioritized Response," *Foreign Affairs*, vol. 83, May/June 2004, p. 132. See also "International: Atrocities Beyond Words," *Economist*, May 3, 2008, vol. 387, p. 69.

3. See Lawrence M. Wein, "Biological and Chemical Safety Nets," *Wall Street Journal*, February 27, 2007, p. A17. See also "A Radioactive Subject," *Economist*, February 3, 2007, p. 60. See also Frank Barnaby, *How to Build a Nuclear Bomb*, Granta Publications, London, 2003.

4. See David P. Auerswald, "Determining Non-State WMD Attacks," *Political Science Quarterly*, vol. 121, no. 4, Winter 2006–2007, p. 543.

5. See "Asia: The Bulldozer Scrapes Home South Korea's Presidential Election," *Economist*, August 25, 2007, p. 56.

6. See Dick Lugar and Sam Nunn, "The New Nuclear Threat," *Wall Street Journal*, August 18, 2007, p. A6.

7. See Thomas B. Cochran and Mathew G. McKinzie, "Detecting Nuclear Smuggling," *Scientific American*, April 2008, p. 98.

8. See William Langewiesche, *The Atomic Bazaar*, Farrar, Straus & Giroux, New York, 2007, p. 71. See also book reviews, *Physics Today*, April 2008, p. 72.

9. In May 2003, North Korea threatened to sell plutonium to the highest bidder. See Michael A. Levi, "Deterring Nuclear Terrorism," *Issues in Science & Technology*, vol. 20, Spring 2004, p. 70.

10. See Martin E. Hellman, "Risk Analysis of Nuclear Deterrence," *The Bent of Tau Beta Pi*, Spring 2008, p. 14.

11. See Graham Allison, *Nuclear Terrorism: The Ultimate Preventable Catastrophe*, Henry Holt, New York, 2004, p. 130.

12. See Niall Ferguson, "One Strike, Iran Could Be Out," *Los Angeles Times*, October 22, 2007.

13. See George P. Shultz, William J. Perry, Henry A. Kissinger, and Sam Nunn, "A World Free of Nuclear Weapons," *Wall Street Journal*, January 4, 2007, p. A15.

CHAPTER TWELVE

1. See *Public Support for U.S. Military Operations*, RAND, Santa Monica, Calif., March 1996.

2. Robert Wood of Harvard University is working to develop a microrobotic fly. See *Time*, October 22, 2007, p. 18. Also see Robert Wood, "Anatomy of a Robotic Fly," *IEEE Spectrum*, March 2008, p. 26.

3. See *BusinessWeek*, September 3, 2007, p. 8.

4. These are rapidly being developed. See *Economist*, November 3, 2007, p. 18. Of course, the means would have to be included to prevent the robot birds from falling into the wrong hands. Coding and other control techniques are quite conceivable to meet this requirement.

CHAPTER THIRTEEN

1. See Richard A. Kerr, "Even Oil Optimists Expect Energy Demand to Outstrip Supply," *Science*, vol. 317, July 27, 2007, p. 437.

2. Not all experts agree. See Vijay V. Vaitheeswaran, "Think Again: Oil," *Foreign Policy*, November/December 2007, p. 25. Also see "The World Has Plenty of Oil," *Wall Street Journal*, March 4, 2008, p. A17.

3. See Frank Zarb, "How to Win the Energy War," *New York Times*, May 23, 2007, p. A23.

4. Increasing by one mile per gallon the performance of all U.S. cars would decrease daily foreign oil imports by 350,000 barrels. See Amy Myers Jaffe, "The Problem: Flip the Switch," *Foreign Policy*, May/June 2007, p. 44.

5. See "Low Carbon Technologies," *Issues in Science and Technology*, National Academy of Engineering, Washington, D.C., Spring 2007, p. 4.

6. See Mathew L. Wald, "Coal's Energy Potential," *New York Times*, May 1, 2007, and John Deutsch and Ernest Montz, "A Future for Fossil Fuel," *Wall Street Journal*, March 15, 2007, p. A17.

7. See Gwyneth Cravens, *Power to Save the World*, Knopf, New York, 2007.

8. See Robert F. Service, "Jay Keasling Profile: Rethinking Mother Nature's Choices," *Science*, vol. 315, February 9, 2007, p. 793. See also "Science and Technology: One for the Road Chemical and Biological Engineering," *Economist*, June 23, 2007, p. 89.

9. See James Tiedje and Timothy Donohue, "Microbes in the Energy Grid," *Science*, vol. 230, May 23, 2008, p. 985.

10. See George A. Olah, "Beyond Oil and Gas: The Methanol Economy," *Angewandte Chemie—International Edition*, vol. 44, 2005, p. 2636.

11. A steady high oil price encourages exploration and drilling in previously less economic regions like deep water and deep underground areas.

12. See "Special Report on Energy Future," *Economist*, June 21, 2008, p. 60.

CHAPTER FOURTEEN

1. See Stuart F. Brown, "Meet the SuperGrid," *Fortune*, August 8, 2005, vol. 152, p. 31.

2. See William Tucker, "Our Atomic Future," *Wall Street Journal*, March 28, 2007, p. A16.

3. See "Zap! You're Not Dead," *Economist*, September 8, 2007, p. 13. See also Gwyneth Cravens, *Power to Save the World*, Knopf, New York, 2007.

4. See "Europe: Nuclear Fallout Energy in Germany," *Economist*, August 4, 2007, p. 43.

5. See Joseph J. Romm, "The Hype about Hydrogen," *Science & Technology*, no. 5, Spring 2004, p. 74.

6. James Hodgson, then secretary of labor.

7. The Interstate Highway System project was huge. See Michael Korda, *Ike: An American Hero*, HarperCollins, New York, 2007, pp. 718–719: "The Interstate Highway System—one of the greatest achievements of Eisenhower's presidency—a public works project so large in scale that it eclipsed everything before or since."

8. The American Interstate Highway System took some 37 years to complete and, in 2006 dollars, cost $425 billion. It is considered to have paid off handsomely in productivity gains for the nation. See *Economist*, February 16, 2008, p. 12.

9. See Phillip E. Tatlock and Michael Oppenheimer, "The Boundaries of the Thinkable," *Daedalus*, Spring 2008, p. 64.

CHAPTER FIFTEEN

1. See the several articles in the spring 2008 issue of the National Academy of Engineering's *The Bridge*.

2. A system of this kind, one that could impact the health of the citizenry, might of course generate unforeseen legal barriers.

CHAPTER SIXTEEN

1. In September 2007, the Saudi Interior Ministry announced the setting up of a special force to guard the country's oil facilities against possible terror attacks. See "The World This Week," *Economist* (London), September 1, 2007, vol. 384, p. 6.
2. Many younger Saudis do indeed possess such academic degrees from U.S. and British universities, and some have even had training with the U.S. Air Force.

|Index

|About the Authors

Simon Ramo received a Ph.D. degree magna cum laude from the California Institute of Technology. A pioneer in electronics research and development, he was awarded the National Medal of Science by President Carter. Ramo has been a leader in developing technology for national defense, becoming the chief scientist and technical director of the United States' largest defense program, the intercontinental ballistic missile (ICBM). He received the Presidential Medal of Freedom, the United States' highest civilian award, from President Reagan.

A founder and principal executive of several successful high-tech companies including TRW Inc. (Thompson Ramo Wooldridge), he has been inducted into the Business Hall of Fame. Ramo's textbooks in science, engineering, and management have been translated into numerous foreign languages and are used in universities throughout the world. His *Extraordinary Tennis for the Ordinary Player* holds the sales record for books on tennis.

Ronald D. Sugar is chairman of the board and chief executive officer of the Northrop Grumman Corporation. He was previously president of Litton Industries Inc., president of TRW Aerospace, and chief financial officer of TRW Inc. He is past chairman of the U.S. Aerospace Industries Association and serves as a director on corporate, university, cultural, and charitable institution boards.

Sugar is a summa cum laude graduate of the University of California, Los Angeles, from which institution he received a doctorate degree in engineering and was honored as Engineering Alumnus of the Year. He is a member of the National Academy of Engineering, a fellow of the Royal Aeronautical Society, and a fellow of the American Institute of Aeronautics and Astronautics. He was appointed by President Clinton to the National Security Telecommunications Advisory Committee. He is the recipient of the Marine Corps Foundation's Semper Fidelis Award and the Air Force Association's John R. Alison Award for Industrial Leadership in National Defense.